On Becoming Shryock

To order additional copies of
On Becoming Shryock,
by
Richard A. Schaefer,
call
1-800-765-6955.

Visit us at
www.reviewandherald.com
for information on other Review and Herald® products.

On Becoming **Shryock**

A

Life

of Surprise

and Inspiration

Richard A. Schaefer

REVIEW AND HERALD® PUBLISHING ASSOCIATION
HAGERSTOWN, MD 21741-1119

This book was
Edited by Patricia Lance Fritz
Interior design by Candy Harvey
Cover design by Trent Truman
Electronic makeup by Shirley M. Bolivar
Typeset: Bembo 11/14

PRINTED IN U.S.A.

09 08 07 06 05   5 4 3 2 1

R&H Cataloging Service
Schaefer, Richard A.
    On Becoming Shryock: A life of surprise and inspiration.

    1. Shryock, Edwin Harold, 1906-2004. 2. Loma Linda University. Medical School—History. 3. Medicine—Study and teaching—Seventh-day Adventists—Biographies. I. Title.

[B]

ISBN 978-0-8280-1889-0

Dedicated to the student physicians
of the Loma Linda University School of Medicine

Acknowledgments

A project of the Heritage Room at Loma Linda University, this book is the personal story of E. Harold Shryock, M.D. His life provides a unique perspective on the early days of the Loma Linda Sanitarium and the College of Medical Evangelists, which became Loma Linda University Medical Center and the Loma Linda University School of Medicine.

The manuscript has benefited immeasurably from the valuable participation of Shryock and his children, Patti Wallace and Dr. Ed Shryock. The Shryock family remained open and candid in their participation as the manuscript evolved.

Our story developed from a variety of sources: oral histories, church and university publications and records, and personal conversations.

Over the course of 18 months, I often sought clarification from Shryock, sometimes daily. He shared his personal files with me. We ate together, laughed together, and prayed together. We drove around Loma Linda, talking about facilities and people from the past. In the process, we became friends.

Shryock insisted that this book feature the combined providences he experienced during his lifetime as well as those divine interventions that formed and shaped Loma Linda University, the institution he served for 41 years. He also insisted that any wisdom demonstrated on his part be attributed to the Bible and the writings of Ellen G. White.

Consultants included: contributing editor Charles Mills; Edna Maye Loveless, Ph.D., retired chair of the English and Communication Department at La Sierra University; Lisa M. Beardsley, Ph.D., vice chancellor for academic affairs, Loma Linda University; and Merlin D. Burt,

Ph.D., at the time, chair of the Department of Archives and Special Collections, Loma Linda University. The book has benefited immeasurably from their time and counsel. Others contributed to this project. Carolyn Thompson, R.N., produced "A Conversation With Harold Shryock," hosted by David R. Larson, Ph.D., as part of the Adventist Heritage Series. Donald L. Anderson, M.D., also videotaped an oral history with Shryock. (Anderson's father, Godfrey T. Anderson, Ph.D., was the president of the College of Medical Evangelists when it became Loma Linda University.) I especially thank Trish Chapman, Petre Cimpoeru, Colleen Doran, and Janice Little, the staff of the Department of Archives and Special Collections who routinely provided valuable assistance. May our collective efforts in telling Shryock's fascinating story provide inspiration for generations to come.

Contents

Foreword

riting this book has been a privilege, an honor, and an inspiration. The name Harold Shryock, M.D., is well known in Seventh-day Adventist circles. His writings have encompassed the globe for 70 years, and his contributions to the Seventh-day Adventist Church and Loma Linda University School of Medicine are legendary. Many know the man from what he wrote, how he taught and administered, and what he said. Few know his incredible personal story and the profound influence it had on his many contributions.

Loma Linda's pioneers were real people. They fought the good fight of faith in spite of human frailties. This story's fascinating insights into the less-than-perfect development of the Seventh-day Adventist Church's medical outreach promise that we, too, can contribute to God's cause despite our human shortcomings.

Events that seemed problematic throughout much of his life, Shryock eventually recognized as providential. Yes, he acknowledged a cloud or two, but he always pointed to the light behind the cloud. The trials he encountered, and the personal growth he experienced as a result, contributed immeasurably to his ministry.

This book chronicles Shryock's experiences from his days as an ailing youth to his successes as a respected medical educator, college administrator, author, counselor, and public speaker. It's also a touching love story.

I pray that you'll find this book to be representative of the man as well as informative, entertaining, and most of all, inspirational.

—Richard A. Schaefer

Prologue

t's after midnight. Harold Shryock, M.D., an intern at the Loma Linda Sanitarium and Hospital, is about to undergo an experience that will impact the rest of his life.

An unconscious young woman with multiple injuries has just been transported to the facility. Involved in a deadly high-speed collision, she lies on a gurney in shock. The attendants smell alcohol on her breath. Shryock shakes his head. "Another pathetic case," he says with a sigh. "The kind that leaves doctors and nurses feeling helpless because there's so little we can do to save a life."

The woman's injuries include shattered bones and deep lacerations. Her condition appears hopeless. Her two companions have already died from the accident, and the doctors don't expect her to live more than a few hours.

The patient's insurance company orders her to be transferred to Los Angeles. As preparations are being made, Harold monitors the woman's vital signs.

Suddenly, she opens an unbandaged eye and looks around the room. She even tries to speak. Though her mind isn't clear, it seems she might regain consciousness. As in all cases like this, next of kin must be notified. Someone needs to ask her how to reach them.

Frank "Monty" Montgomery, a nurse, steps in. Because of his many years of experience dealing with such sensitive situations, nurses and interns alike look to Monty for help. Unknowingly, Harold is about to learn something profound regarding life's priorities from a man without any impressive degrees behind his name—someone not even on the faculty of the institution. Harold is about to see, firsthand, personal ministry that's generally understood to be part of the hospital's mission, but wasn't included in Harold's formal education or job description.

Monty immediately senses the situation is grave. Wasting no time on preliminaries, he approaches the patient, takes her hand, and says in a quiet, even voice, "You've been in an accident and are badly hurt. Your mother will want to know where you are. Will you share with me your mother's name and address?"

The youthful patient moves slightly, opens her eye again, and looks into Monty's face. "Is that *all* you want to tell Mother?" she asks.

Monty senses that the woman wants to spare her mother the anguish of knowing that the accident had occurred while her precious daughter was intoxicated.

After Monty's reassurance, the patient whispers the information. Then, without pause or timidity, he asks the woman if she believes in prayer. The young woman opens her eye again and whispers, "Mother does."

"Would you like me to get the minister and some of the doctors to come in and have prayer with you?"

The patient's lips quiver as she nods her head slightly and squeezes Monty's hand. He leaves the room and soon returns with the chaplain and a doctor. Harold joins them; they arrange themselves around the bed and reverently bow their heads, as Monty offers a simple prayer, asking their heavenly Father for mercy and praying that His will might prevail.

The young woman dies within hours of arriving in Los Angeles.

A few days after the incident, Monty approached Harold in the hallway. "I think that girl's mother—the girl that we prayed for just before she left the hospital—would like to have us come and see her and tell her that we had prayed with her daughter."

Harold nodded his head. "That's a good idea, Monty. Let's do it this weekend."

The next Sabbath the two men and their wives drove into Los Angeles, to the address whispered by the dying woman. As soon as they were all seated in the mother's living room, Monty spoke, great emotion affecting his voice. "We're so sorry about the recent loss of your daughter," he said quietly. "Dr. Shryock here and I were part of the team that helped take care of her out in Loma Linda. Would you . . . would you like us to tell you about what happened that night?"

The mother lifted her hand. "I met the ambulance when my daughter arrived in Los Angeles. I . . . I already know what happened at Loma Linda. She was conscious for a little while, and . . . and the first thing she said was, 'Mother, those Loma Linda people were good to me. They prayed for me because I'd been hurt so badly.'"

Later, on the way home, Monty, who, under the Spirit's guidance, had brought many to conversion, expressed his feelings. "You never can tell how much good it does to pray with a person," he said soberly. "We can't tell whether or not that girl gave her heart to God. We won't know until the judgment day whether she accepted forgiveness for her wayward life. But even if our prayers didn't do any good for the daughter, I'm sure it comforted the mother to know that we prayed with her child, and that she remembered the prayer."

After many years of observation, Harold considered Monty a mentor and hero. His ability to make a person see the bright side of life inspired Harold. He possessed an unusual gift of humor, which he used to help patients deal with pain, teach student nurses how to relate to patients, and even keep one intern from becoming too self-sufficient.

Monty Montgomery impacted Harold Shryock's life in profound ways. Throughout his career, Shryock incorporated his friend's unique brand of compassion, humor, creativity, fearless integrity, and spirituality. When he began counseling young people, many of whom had serious problems adjusting to professional school, Harold decided to end each session with prayer. In a broader sense, prayer became an important part of his personal ministry at The College of Medical Evangelists (CME) in Loma Linda, California. Monty had become Harold's role model—a symbol of the best of CME, a symbol that he himself would come to exemplify.

＜

The history of CME and the life story of Harold Shryock are intriguingly intermingled. By age 97, Shryock had been an eyewitness to every class in the School of Medicine. In both his story and that of CME, challenges, frustrations, questionable potential, human interest, and amazing accomplishments spotlight the work of divine intervention.

Harold Shryock had to overcome youthful handicaps that easily could have held him back for his entire life. After making courageous adjustments to his early life challenges, after tolerating unprecedented delays in beginning his medical career, after almost being killed in an accidental electrocution, and after making daring decisions regarding his own destiny, Shryock matured, and eventually accepted enormous professional responsibilities.

Harold Shryock, M.D., worked for 41 years at the institution known today as Loma Linda University. He became a professor and chair of the Department of Anatomy and dean of the School of Medicine. He wrote 621 magazine articles and 13 books. A public speaker at church, school, and alumni meetings across the United States and Canada, as a physician he spoke to as many as 10,000 people at a time. He counseled hundreds of college students regarding scholastic, financial, and marital issues. And in a quest for the most qualified applicants, he overhauled the admissions procedures for what became the Loma Linda University School of Medicine.

According to H. Roger Hadley, M.D., current dean, Shryock set the standards for recruiting students. He established admissions policies by developing innovative ways of assessing premedical students, determining how letters of recommendation would be written and interpreted, and conducting on-campus interviews. He became the first dean to routinely visit Seventh-day Adventist undergraduate campuses throughout the United States, something subsequent deans have continued to do.

His refinements and untiring efforts to determine the best-qualified applicants opened doors of opportunity and service to hundreds of potential physicians.

Harold Shryock, M.D., joined 11 medical societies, was listed in Who's Who in America, and received Alumnus of the Year honors at two institutions of higher education.

His life achievements are noteworthy not only because of their numbers and valuable contributions but, even more incredibly, because of limitations he overcame in order to achieve them.

While endeavoring to balance devotion to God, family, and career, he contributed to the physical, mental, and spiritual well-being of countless members of the Seventh-day Adventist Church and of the public.

Most important, Harold Shryock recognized and answered God's callings. As a result, he made bold, creative, and unparalleled contributions to Loma Linda University, one of the greatest ventures of faith in the history of Christian outreach. In the minds of his students and colleagues, Harold became a giant among men.

This is his story.

Chapter 1

Papa Joins a One-horse Medical School

Providential intervention, often recognized at the moment it occurs, is sometimes not identified, however, until a series of events have been observed over time. In some situations, certain occurrences, with no particular connection with elements that don't even seem to make sense, are acknowledged years later as acts of Providence.

The story of Harold Shryock, intermingled as it is with the history of Loma Linda University, represents just such a case. Divine intervention at Loma Linda can't fully be appreciated without understanding the story of both as they weave within the folds of time. And that perspective must include the profound influences of Alfred Quimby Shryock and Stella Louisa Shryock—Harold's talented, well-educated, and dedicated parents.

Alfred Shryock, reared on a farm in Iowa, was an 1899 graduate of the American Medical Missionary College (AMMC) in Battle Creek, Michigan. The medical school, affiliated with the world-famous Battle Creek Sanitarium, operated under the sometimes eccentric but always fascinating direction of John Harvey Kellogg, M.D.

Stella, whose father worked for the railroad in Indiana, completed the sanitarium's nurse-training course just before the couple married that same year. Both were second-generation Adventists.

Alfred, president of his senior class, was now a practicing physician. He believed helping people was more important than gaining wealth, a philosophy that had a major impact on Harold.

After teaching for one year at AMMC, Alfred accepted an invitation from the Washington Conference of Seventh-day Adventists to direct a church-owned hydrotherapy treatment unit. He moved the hydrotherapy unit to a better location, installed Stella as supervisor and receptionist, and eventually employed several other nurses and a "lady physician."[1] The unit flourished as it treated patients suffering from upper respiratory infections. Just as the hydrotherapy unit began to grow, so did the Shryock family. Edwin Harold Shryock made his 9-pound appearance on April 14, 1906, after a prolonged home delivery. Alfred was 34; Stella was 30.

Babies often were delivered at home at the turn of the century. Alfred employed a lady physician, M. L. Allison, to attend Stella for the difficult delivery at the couple's small but cozy home, located at 410 Malden Avenue, in Seattle.

Harold had no formal birth certificate. Instead, his father mailed a post-card-sized "Birth Return" from the City of Seattle Department of Sanitation to King County, citing the essential facts of his son's birth. It included, among other pertinent information, that Harold was "legitimate." A photo-copy of this document served as Harold's birth certificate through the years.

While Stella favored administrative work over homemaking, little Harold's arrival shifted her priorities in a hurry. She decided to bottle feed her baby. But commercially prepared formulas were not yet available, so she and Alfred improvised a formula using evaporated milk as a principle ingredient. Harold didn't seem to mind, and he grew rapidly. He called his parents "Mama" and "Papa" and went everywhere with them. Some observers of his mother's constant, loving attentions toward her firstborn considered him "spoiled."

By 1908 Alfred had prospered. He'd established a substantial family medicine practice associated with the hydrotherapy unit and built a new home on Queen Anne Hill, a residential suburb of Seattle. Life was both fulfilling and enjoyable for the little family.

⌒

When Harold was about 2½ years old, the Shryocks spent their winter vacation touring some of the Seventh-day Adventist sanitariums being developed in southern California. They visited St. Helena Sanitarium in the Napa Valley, as well as new sanitariums in National City, Glendale, and Loma Linda.

Because of its controversial roots, church members considered Loma Linda Sanitarium to be of special interest. Some even called its launch sensational.

Ellen G. White, one of the founders of the Seventh-day Adventist denomination, exercised a profound influence on the establishment of Loma Linda Sanitarium. Members of the Adventist Church considered Mrs. White, by now an elderly widow, a prophetess—the "Lord's messenger." Amazing fulfillments of her predictions convinced many that Providence not only was directing the Sanitarium's establishment; Providence was also directing her. From her home near St. Helena, Mrs. White made a daring pronouncement that set the stage for Loma Linda University's providential heritage. She predicted that unoccupied properties, on which buildings were already erected, in localities especially suited to sanitarium work, would "be offered to us at much less than their original cost" (*E. G. White Letter 157,* October 13, 1902).

"Some . . . will in God's providence invest their means to develop properties and erect buildings," she wrote. "In time, these properties will be offered for sale at a price far below their cost. Our people will recognize the hand of Providence in these offers and will secure valuable properties for use in institutional work."

How did this prophecy relate to Loma Linda? Not much, at first.

On October 10, 1901, Ellen White had described a southern California property she saw in a vision of the night. In her journal, she wrote that she seemed to be living there, and described patients sitting in wheelchairs, outdoors, under shade trees that seemed to form tentlike canopies. (*The Story of Our Health Message,* p. 343.) While fulfilling the prophecy that the church would be offered appropriate properties at much less than their original cost, the two buildings the church had already purchased did not match this vivid image. *That place must still be located!* Although she did not yet know it, Loma Linda matched her vision: an institution with great trees forming a massive canopy.

A year earlier, on September 29, 1900, the Loma Linda Association, a well-financed group of 40 businessmen and 80 physicians, filed its articles of incorporation, announcing its intention to operate a sanitarium and hospital. Its qualified and financially capable stockholders and officers included bank presidents, hotel proprietors, a utility company president, a hospital manager, an attorney, and the chief examiner, in Los Angeles, for several national insurance companies.

On October 6, 1900, the group purchased an area on the south side of the San Bernardino valley known as Mound City. Resting on the property sat a failed luxury hotel. By 1902, the organization had named the place "Loma Linda" and was in the process of creating a 90-room healthcare resort five miles west of Redlands. The facility was well equipped, staffed, and funded. Loma Linda was not even close to being put on the market. At that time, it certainly didn't fit the description in Mrs. White's 1902 statement regarding properties that would "be offered to us at much less than their original cost."

But, in 1904, Ellen White asked church members to look in the areas of Riverside, San Bernardino, and Redlands for property that she had seen in vision. In May 1905, John Burden, an Adventist who'd been manager of St. Helena Sanitarium and who had promoted sanitarium work in Australia and southern California, reported 76 acres of land that matched her description . . . almost.

After the Loma Linda Association had invested $155,000 in new buildings, redecorating, furnishings, and other improvements, their venture failed. For months Loma Linda had been deserted except for a caretaker and grazing sheep. When Burden inquired about the price, he learned that the property could be purchased for $110,000. The price was eventually lowered to $85,000 and, eventually, dropped to an incredible $40,000. Finally, in 1905, Loma Linda perfectly fit Mrs. White's 1902 description.

With her urgent direction ringing in his ears and knowing that others were interested in buying the recently depreciated property, Burden decided to purchase the land and buildings.

The terms were simple: $5,000 down followed by three monthly payments of $5,000 each; the remaining $20,000 was to be paid at the end of three years.

On Friday afternoon, May 26, 1905, lawyers arrived to sign the contract of sale. But, because it was nearing sunset and the Sabbath hours were about to begin, Burden and the few church members with him decided to postpone the signing of the papers until the following Monday.

That Sunday, May 28, Burden received a telegram from G. W. Reaser, the new president of the Southern California Conference, who, at the time, was at the church headquarters in Takoma Park, Maryland. The message read, "Developments here warrant advising do not make deposit on sanitarium." But heeding Mrs. White's urging instead, and with her assurance that the Lord would provide, Burden went ahead and paid the $1,000 on Monday to secure an option to buy Loma Linda. He'd forfeit the money if the deal fell through.

Two weeks later, on Monday morning, June 12, 1905, an express wagon arrived bringing Mrs. White to the Loma Linda property for her first visit. As she made her inspection tour, she'd point, and say, "This is the very place I saw in vision."

Then, seating herself in the recreation hall with about 20 faithful friends and coworkers gathered about her, she spoke of the great educational work that someday would be carried forward in Loma Linda.

However, in spite of clear evidence that God was leading, financial realities loomed large before the church constituency. That evening, voices were raised saying, "If the present owners, with all of their talent and resources, had failed in their efforts to operate a health-care institution in Loma Linda, what should lead the church to think that they could succeed at doing the same thing?"

Nevertheless, encouraged by faith in Ellen White's testimony and in her conviction that Loma Linda was to play a role in God's work, local Adventists contributed the remaining $4,000 to complete the June 15 down payment. No one had any idea how they'd meet the July note—another $5,000.

Finally, the Southern California Conference Committee agreed to support the project. But, during the following weeks, no money arrived.

On July 26, 1905, the due date of the second payment, the conference committee met with Burden in Los Angeles in an emergency session. The meeting started at 9:00 a.m. The payment was due at 2:00 p.m.

"We don't have the $5,000," the committee members declared.

"How much do you have?" Burden asked.

"None of it."

Some in the room even criticized Burden for following so blindly the counsel of an old woman. But the man refused to admit defeat. "Mrs. White has told me that the money will come from unexpected sources," he declared. "We must be patient and wait for God's leading."

The 10:00 a.m. mail included a letter from a woman in Atlantic City, New Jersey. Nobody on the committee knew anything about her, nor were they expecting the letter that had just traveled across the continent. When they opened the envelope, eyes blinked in disbelief. Tucked inside was a bank draft for $5,000,[2] the *exact* amount needed four hours later on that deadline day. One of Ellen White's unexpected sources had come through just in time.

Incredibly, other unexpected funds from various persons made it possible to pay for the Loma Linda property in less than six months, thus gaining additional discounts totaling $1,100. The final purchase price was $38,900— much less than its original cost; and the money came from unexpected sources, for unoccupied property that had a tentlike canopy of trees.

This controversial, yet providential beginning of the institution motivated Alfred and Stella Shryock to visit Loma Linda during their swing through the southern portion of the state. Most of the institution's five full-time physicians had been Alfred's schoolmates at AMMC. They expressed their strong faith that their new institution was operating under a divine mandate and announced that they were about to organize a school of medicine. "Alfred, you must come and join the faculty," they pleaded.

They based their wide-ranging plans on Ellen White's recent statement that "physicians are to receive their education here," an incredibly ambitious declaration, considering that the sanitarium still struggled for existence.

George K. Abbott, M.D., a 1903 graduate of AMMC and superintendent of the Loma Linda Sanitarium, remembered that Alfred Shryock had had some teaching experience, and urged him to come and join the team. He specifically expressed his need for an instructor in histology and human embryology. Shryock had worked for Dr. A. B. Olson at AMMC as a student laboratory assistant for a course in histology.

On their way back to Seattle, Alfred thought long and hard about the invitation. By the time they arrived home, he'd rejected the whole idea of successfully starting a school of medicine. "It's an unrealistic hope," he told Stella. "I don't care to be affiliated with a one-horse medical school."

Nevertheless, the physicians at Loma Linda proved strongly motivated and persistent. They continued their appeal by mail. "We believe the plan to develop a school here for the training of gospel medical missionary evangelists is divinely ordained," they wrote.

Although the Shryocks were favorably impressed with the Loma Linda physicians' sincerity, they were not persuaded. John Burden, now business manager at Loma Linda, offered Shryock a salary of $20 per week. When Alfred replied that he would be unable to meet his fixed expenses on $20 per week, Burden replied that after due consideration he'd up the ante to $21 a week.

Trying to remain conscientious, the Shryocks thought, "Maybe the Lord's hand is in this." So they prayed for a sign. If God wanted them to move to Loma Linda, He'd send a buyer for their new home. Yes, the couple agreed, that certainly would be an impressive indicator.

Alfred listed his property with a realtor on his way to work one morning. The house sold before noon, and by sundown it was in escrow. In Alfred and Stella's minds, Providence had made it perfectly clear what direction their future would take.

Shryock moved his small family to southern California and became Loma Linda's sixth physician.

The little family arrived by train at the Loma Linda depot on New Year's Day, 1910—about three months after the first freshman class had enrolled and within three weeks of the December 9, 1909, incorporation of the College of Medical Evangelists (CME).

A 119-step grand stairway led up the north slope of the hill to the sanitarium's main entrance. In nearby fields, horses pulled farm implements.

When patients arrived by steam locomotive, the sanitarium would send a horse and buggy to meet them. The buggy was waiting when Alfred, Stella, and almost-4-year-old Harold's train chugged into the station.

"I am from the sanitarium," called a young driver, stepping forward in greeting. "May I help you?"

"Yes, we're looking for Dr. George Abbott," stated Alfred. "We are in the process of moving here. I've come to be a teacher in the new medical school."

The young man loaded the Shryocks and their luggage onto the horse-drawn carriage and soon drove the family up the steep, curved driveway, heading for the rear entrance of the sanitarium to find Abbott.

"Where are the streetcars?" little Harold asked, eyeing the activity going on around them.

we don't have any streetcars here," replied the driver.

"But how do you go downtown?"

"We don't have a downtown."

"But . . ." Harold pressed, "how will my mother do her shopping?"

"When a woman wants to go shopping," the driver explained, "she has to go to San Bernardino or Redlands."

"I don't like it here," Harold said with a pout. "I like streetcars."

Alfred interrupted the conversation with a touch on his son's arm. "Harold, your toys will be coming when our furniture arrives from Seattle. Then you'll like it here just fine." Harold was not convinced and grew silent as the buggy pulled up to the back of the old hotel.

John Burden welcomed the Shryocks as soon as they entered the foyer. The facility was not only a health-care institution; it was also the town's civic center, complete with post office and cashier. Later, when telephone lines began to be strung around the town, the community switchboard took up residence in the sanitarium, too.

"I've reserved a four-room bungalow for you on Pepper Drive," Burden explained with an eager handshake. "You're welcome to stay in the sanitarium and eat in the patients' dining room until your household goods arrive."

The Shryocks' four-room bungalow stood among a row of houses owned and maintained by CME about one quarter mile north of the hill on what is now Anderson Street. It boasted a front room, dining room, kitchen, and one bedroom. Although it provided indoor plumbing, it had no electricity, no gas for cooking or heating, and no telephone. A wood stove promised heat for the often chilly southern California winters. Water for bathing had to be heated on the wood stove. Oil lamps threw a dim, shadowy light; a kerosene stove provided a fire for cooking.

In 1914 Harold's father and a partner purchased a used Model-T Ford, one of only a few vehicles in Loma Linda at the time. This handy conveyance suddenly classed him and his partner among Loma Linda's elite. The vehicle's one taillight and two windshield lights were kerosene lamps. The much brighter headlights were powered by acetylene gas. All needed to be lit with a match. The acetylene gas was created by a carbide generator, a round cylinder mounted on the driver's side running board. Carbide crystals (located in the bottom of the generator), which had to be replaced regularly, would release the flammable gas when drops of water fell on them. Rubber tubes carried the gas to each headlight. The normal motion of the car would automatically cause the water to drop periodically on the carbide crystals. But when the vehicle became stationary, Harold would keep the water drops falling by pounding on the side of the generator's water tank. If he didn't, the headlights would go out.

Young Harold would sometimes sit on the passenger's side of the front seat and imagine himself a sort of co-pilot. One afternoon on Baseline Avenue in San Bernardino, when Alfred was feeling a bit adventuresome, he accelerated the Model-T to its exhilarating top speed of 25 mph. After their need for speed was satisfied, Alfred and Harold slowed to the normal cruising velocity of 15 mph.

The institution had not yet invested in motorized transportation. Supplies for the sanitarium bakery and store arrived by steam locomotive and were unloaded at a special siding on the south side of the tracks, just west of the Pepper Drive railroad crossing. The store was open seven days a week, including Saturday evenings. It was a gathering place. Everyone knew everyone else in the small community.

Even before the School of Medicine was incorporated, CME became the talk of the town, when, in October 1909, 10 medical students enrolled in its first class. Six graduated from the five-year curriculum in 1914.

In those early days, faculty members carried multiple responsibilities. Abbott, the president of CME, taught hydrotherapy. Archibald W. Truman, M.D., held forth in physiology and anatomy classes and saw patients in the sanitarium. Edward H. Risley, M.D., opened to his students the wonders of physiological chemistry while serving as director of the X-ray room. Julia A. White, M.D., instructed in obstetrics and gynecology and administered the nurses' training school.

Alfred taught not only histology and human embryology, but also ran the pharmacy and drew blood from patients needing blood chemistries. W. A. George, M.D., who arrived a year after Alfred, performed surgery and taught gross anatomy. His wife, Lyra, also a physician, administered anesthesia for her husband's surgical patients and also delivered babies.

It's amazing that this small group of brave family physicians could even presume that they would be successful in starting a medical school. But each was conscientiously committed to the enterprise.

＠

Harold remembered that Ellen White came to Loma Linda several times between 1910 and 1915. The institutional family considered her visits as special events. Every time she'd arrive, a holiday feeling would sweep over the hill, and all would gather to listen to what she had to say. She had determined to speak to her "family" of workers and students and to address the entire Seventh-day Adventist church group for as long as her strength allowed.

Everyone walking the corridors and occupying the patient-care facilities and busy classrooms believed that the institution had been divinely established and providentially guided by counsels given through Ellen White. And everyone considered John Burden to be Mrs. White's representative at Loma Linda. This perception, combined with his very clear example of personal self-denial, contributed to an almost palpable spirit of unity and loyalty throughout the institution.

The Burdens occupied a room at the sanitarium. They knew all the patients personally. They appeared to be on duty 24 hours a day, seven days a week. Nothing escaped their notice. As manager, John Burden could show up anywhere, any time. His administrative style was simple, but effective.

Salaries for workers were $12 to $20 a week. Even though their incomes were inadequate, manager Burden encouraged his personnel to contribute to benevolent projects. He had ways of maintaining morale and encouraging employees to persist, even under hardships. Whenever institutional income was insufficient to meet payroll, he suffered along with everyone else.

Employees were called "helpers," and it became a tradition every autumn for the institutional family to meet out on the lawn in what were called "Helper's Meetings." Helpers were fascinated and inspired as they listened to Burden tell the stories of how he'd followed Mrs. White's counsel in the founding of the institution, even against his own better judgment.

Each story recounting God's providences further strengthened Alfred's conviction that connecting with CME had been the right thing to do. His meager facilities included a small laboratory and a few microscopes located in a room in the Assembly Hall—the former Loma Linda Resort's recreation hall, a rustic, imitation-log building located near the middle of the present site of Nichol Hall. Shryock labored without any secretarial or technical help whatsoever.

The course he taught included instructing medical students how to prepare their own slides for study under the microscope.

Shryock did have one part-time employee: Willie Joseph, a local teenager who knew the countryside, was given the job of helping him find frogs in the evenings. Medical students studied blood circulation by holding a frog's foot under the microscope and observing the blood vessels in the thin webbing between the frog's toes.

To teach embryology, Shryock purchased fertilized eggs from local farmers, brought them back to his laboratory, and incubated them. Students studied embryos at various stages of development.

Although the facilities were deficient, the 10 students were sincere and highly motivated. Some came from other countries. Some were quite young, because the five-year, six-day-a-week CME curriculum required only a few prerequisites and could admit students directly from the twelfth grade. Most had part-time jobs. One worked as a telephone operator.

Because the new medical school was a step child of the sanitarium, John Burden oversaw its financial interests, as well. The vitality of CME depended largely on the earnings of the sanitarium. For this reason, the CME administration felt they must respect his opinions.

For example, Burden vigorously opposed any plan to conduct anatomy dissections on campus. "Our patients would surely be upset," he pointed out, "if they thought their bodies would be dissected should they die at the sanitarium." This fear was unfounded, because state legislation controlled medical-school dissections in a program completely unrelated to patients in private institutions. But Burden would not yield. His concern about patients' perceptions led CME to rent a facility in Colton, to which medical students and teachers had to commute several times a week. Some walked the four miles. Others took the train. In time, because of complaints from the local citizenry, Colton city fathers began to object.

Burden finally agreed to the emergency construction of a corrugated sheet metal building on the south bank of the San Timoteo Creek, about a quarter mile east of the Pepper Drive (now Anderson Street) bridge. Soon dubbed "Jericho" by medical students, the building rested on a cement slab and was well obscured by a surrounding orange grove.

In the interest of institutional harmony, Shryock tolerated the inconveniences and conservative opinions he encountered. The family atmosphere on the hill proved pervasive. Aware that the purchase of the property and development of the institution had been providentially guided, students and employees alike considered their involvement a unique and blessed privilege.

---

[1] The term identifying female physicians of the day. Although most physicians at that time were men, CME's first several classes were one third female. Today, half the members of Loma Linda University School of Medicine classes are female.

[2] $100,000 today.

Chapter 2

On Becoming a Man

L oneliness, mischief, educational advantages, a natural disaster, and even a mysterious illness colored Harold Shryock's unique childhood.

At first Mother didn't work outside the home. Bored by the monotony of small village life, Stella felt deprived of the financial security and daily associations she'd enjoyed in Alfred's Seattle practice. Although she was actively involved with church outreach programs in the community, caring for Harold remained her first priority.

The Shryocks decided to homeschool their growing, energetic boy. Although he later acknowledged the good motives of his parents, he said he felt sheltered and isolated, and became quite self-centered. He didn't readily learn the give-and-take in relationships with other people and lacked experience in making his own decisions.

Outwardly, Harold's behavior seemed perfect. His parents saw to that. But, inwardly, conflicting forces troubled him. He tended to be mischievous and had to carefully conceal some of his activities.

For the first seven years of his schooling, Harold studied hard, but indulged in a bit of misbehavior on the side to break the routine. In time young Harold developed interests in sports, bicycling, auto mechanics, and outdoor living. However, wanting their son to become a physician, Mom and Dad channeled Harold's energies into scholastic pursuits and music. Although he did well in both, he grew to resent his parents for insisting that he pursue their interests rather than his own.

Throughout his childhood, he was led to believe that he was special, even superior to others his own age who didn't have the advantages provided by his parents. Harold *did* have advantages. Both parents were intelligent and capable educators. Alfred taught his son the fundamental principles of arithmetic. Stella, who had an excellent background in grammar, taught her offspring literary structure and how to diagram sentences. Even through these simple, homegrown lessons, Providence was working with a sometimes-reluctant student to prepare him for one of his future adult avocations—writing.

When Harold reached the seventh grade, the Shryocks hired a tutor, Mrs. O. J. Graf, to guide him through the rough scholastic waters. When he finally enrolled in the eighth grade, he completed his lesson assignments with ease.

In 1916 a major flood so altered the routine of Loma Linda residents that thereafter all local happenings were described as having occurred "before the flood," or "after the flood." Within a few hours, overflowing rivers and streams established a channel about eight feet deep, running parallel to the railroad tracks. The powerful surge undermined the tracks in places, causing heavy sections of rails and ties to drop to the bottom of the flood channel. The Loma Linda depot washed away. In some places the flood carved a new channel 200 feet wide!

The deluge took a toll on the Shryock family as well. Alfred had just purchased a brand-new 1916 Model T Ford at a cost of almost $400. Unlike his first car, this one had four doors, electric lights, and an electric horn. The floodwaters deposited two feet of silt around the shiny new touring car, burying it up to its axles and running boards. To dig the car out was a major undertaking.

The Shryocks' home, too, filled with mud. Stella became so alarmed by the event that she refused to continue living in the flood-prone area. For a year and a half, the Shryocks moved from one place to another, even taking up residence in two basement rooms of the women's dormitory.

It was here that Mother detected a slight increase in her son's temperature. To be cautious she began keeping a detailed record of Harold's body temperature and noticed that increases occurred in the afternoons and evenings. She had him evaluated by several CME physicians, one of whom thought he detected a heart murmur. Although Alfred himself didn't hear it, Harold was confined to bed for three months. He was told to lie still and not even raise his head. But when nobody was watching, the seventh grader raised his head—just to see if he would die.

Another physician, Newton Evans, later evaluated Harold and concluded that he did not have a heart problem after all. The boy found himself on a strict diet and exercise program similar to those being prescribed for patients with systemic tuberculosis. After being bedridden for three months, he had to learn to walk again, but this new regimen—eating lots of good food and gradually increasing his physical endurance—contributed to his recovery. He enjoyed riding his bicycle to and from school, which helped him regain his strength.

After two additional moves, the Shryocks finally occupied a permanent rental named "Shamrock" on Mound Street (just across from the present-day site of the Loma Linda Market). It was one of the original bungalows that had been moved and enlarged.

As he grew older, Harold enjoyed tinkering with his father's new cars. Model T Fords came with an owner's manual and a set of tools. Alfred allowed his son certain privileges that he considered part of his education. "You can do anything you wish with our family car," Dad declared, "as long you have it in running order when I come home from work." Sitting behind the steering wheel while the vehicle remained safely parked in the garage, Harold fantasized that he was driving the car and racing down the local roads. Thus began Harold's lifelong love affair with the automobile.

Because Alfred was not mechanically inclined, when a connecting-rod bearing on the Model T gave way, he simply quit using the vehicle. Alfred then purchased a relatively new 1918 Dodge touring car from Fred E. Herzer, Sr., M.D. (CME: 1914). The accompanying owner's manual enabled the owner to perform all maintenance and minor repairs, so Alfred entrusted the car's maintenance to his eager and willing son.

Every day Harold anticipated his father's return from work so that the family could take a little ride. Harold became proficient in driving this car, once accelerating to a frightening 35 mph before Dad ordered him to, "Slow down!" Now the family could drive from Loma Linda to San Diego in a mere six hours—provided the tires didn't have to be patched more than two or three times along the way.

Harold began attending a new, 10-grade church school, and entered the eighth grade at age 13. The school was in a one-story building, located on the west side of Pepper Drive (later called Anderson Street), north of the San Timoteo Creek (about a block from today's Redlands Boulevard). Even though he was a newcomer, Harold's schoolmates readily accepted him, and some became long-time personal friends.

The young man headed home as soon as classes ended and spent the rest of his afternoons doing homework or practicing on the piano or cello. This, of course, reduced his contact with the school's organized recreational activities.

During a show-and-tell session at school, Harold demonstrated how to tat (the process of making a netted kind of lace for the border of towels, by looping and knotting strong cotton or linen thread on a hand shuttle). Tatting was something Harold had learned to do while bedridden during his mystery illness. He could tat a yard a day while in bed, a rather unusual skill for a teenage boy.

In 1920 the Southeastern California Conference enlarged the school to 12 grades. About the same time, a four-room, two-story frame structure for high school students rose on the north side of San Timoteo Creek.

Harold landed a few part-time jobs. He became caretaker of the institution's laboratory animals, which included rabbits, guinea pigs, and a goat. Each day, before and after school, he faithfully fed and watered them, and cleaned their cages on Sundays.

Later he labored part-time in the maintenance department, where he developed a great respect for the loyalty and sincerity of CME's carpenters, electricians, plumbers, and welders. Harold remembers that they would assemble each morning for a short worship service before taking up the work of the day.

Those men had a tremendous influence on young Harold Shryock, instilling in him a strong work ethic and a love for the creative process.

Harold also worked as a janitor for a few hours each week, cleaning the medical school buildings. Earning 12 cents an hour, he eventually saved $33, enough to buy a brand-new bicycle from a Redlands bicycle shop.

That same year, when Harold was 14, the Shryock and Risley families vacationed in Yosemite Valley. The trip included a visit to Pacific Union

College (PUC), on Howell Mountain, near St. Helena Sanitarium. During the visit, after seeing the developing facilities and hearing plans for the future, Harold's parents decided that he would someday attend PUC. The Shryocks wanted the best for their son; and the growing college, with its beautiful surroundings, mountaintop location, and capable faculty, represented just that.

Harold Shryock's childhood, impacted by parents so devoted to his potential educational superiority that they didn't adequately prepare him to meet life's normal social challenges, left him an unsuspecting victim of their good intentions.

But one major blessing in his childhood was his ability to find employment. Through hard work, he learned the dignity of labor and how to accept responsibility.

Chapter 3

Ingenuity Strikes

ne word best describes Harold Shryock's high school experience: *Controlled*. Harold's father decided that his son would
complete his studies in just three years by taking extra class
work and attending summer school.

When his 16-year-old offspring was about to start his senior year, a new boarding school called La Sierra Academy (now expanded
to La Sierra University) opened its doors, 20 miles from Loma Linda, near
Riverside. To support the new school, the conference temporarily reduced
Loma Linda Academy to 10 grades, forcing most of Harold's classmates to
continue their Christian education at the new facility.

Harold's father doubted that the Riverside school would be able to
provide the exact subjects his three-year plan required. Also, the
Shryocks weren't ready to trust their son out on his own and living
in a boarding-school dormitory environment. Commuting was out of
the question.

So, after much thought and planning, Alfred enrolled his son in the
secondary school at PUC for the 1922-23 school year. He arranged for
Harold and his mother to live in the community, occupying the second
floor of the home of M. W. Newton, a well-known PUC pioneer and
professor of mathematics and astronomy. "It's a wicked world out there,"
Alfred explained to his not exactly overjoyed son. "Mama will help protect you from the evil influences all around you."

After chugging up Howell Mountain in the family's 1918 Dodge touring car, mother and son arrived at PUC in time for fall classes. But Stella's
health began to deteriorate, forcing Harold to contribute more to her wel-
fare than she did to his. The situation also put a good-sized dent in his so-

cial life. At school-sponsored socials, Harold felt like an outsider, and he kept his few romantic leanings mostly to himself.

When Papa came to visit his family during Thanksgiving, he stopped by the registrar's office and received a bit of a jolt.

"I'm sorry, Doctor," the registrar intoned, glancing over Harold's files, "your son will not graduate next spring."

"Why?" the surprised parent gasped.

"He hasn't had science."

"Well, what science do you teach here?"

The registrar checked the school's class schedule. "The only course of that nature that we're teaching in the academy this year is . . . is . . . physics."

"Then he will join that class," Alfred stated firmly.

"I'm sorry." The registrar sadly shook her head. "That's impossible. You see, the class has been running since school began last fall. It's too late for students to join now. Your son has simply missed too much of the foundation of physics to pick up the course next term."

Circumstances seemed about to derail Papa Shryock's carefully pre-pared three-year plan. He thought for a moment, then brightened. "Listen," he said, "I'm on my way to visit medical schools in Canada, and I'll be back here for Christmas vacation. If I tutor Harold for what the class in physics has covered up until that time, and Professor Mortensen, the physics teacher, gives him an examination that he passes successfully, will you admit him to the course?"

"This is highly irregular," the registrar said with a sigh. "Your son should have been advised at the beginning of the school year that he needed to have a credit in science in order to graduate. But, since you're so adamant about this, and if Harold can catch up with the others, we'll do our best to make an exception in your case."

Harold spent his Christmas vacation studying physics with his father.

To test the latecomer, Professor Mortensen filled three chalkboards with questions. Harold put pen to paper, trying to apply what he'd learned in his holiday crash course. When the dust settled and the examination was graded, Professor Mortensen announced that the boy had passed!

Harold joined the class and completed academy in his third year, ex-actly according to Papa's master plan.

During this time, Harold had been developing some plans of his own.

He became more involved in deciding his own future and wanted to be emancipated from his parents' close supervision. The following summer, before he was to enter college at PUC, Harold respectfully told his dad, "I am not willing to be chaperoned by Mama in activities away from home."

But the Shryocks weren't yet ready to trust Harold with dormitory life and countered with another idea. Harold would become a special student at Loma Linda and live at home with *both* parents. The father's ingenuity had struck.

Still, Providence was at work, even though the results wouldn't be evident for years. Alfred's decision played a far greater role in Harold's future than anyone could have imagined.

The two-year curriculum of Loma Linda's new Dietitians' Training School accepted students straight from high school. Because of a requirement that dietetics students take a course in physiological chemistry during their second year along with freshman medical students, and because they hadn't taken the prerequisite courses in college chemistry, many were forced to attend general and organic chemistry and qualitative analysis classes during their first year.

"Aha!" Alfred triumphed. "Harold can become a special student in the Dietitians' Training School and get his chemistries right here at Loma Linda. And he can take Bible courses with the dietetics students."

Alfred hired Charles Plumb, a medical student at Loma Linda who'd once taught mathematics at Union College in Lincoln, Nebraska, to tutor Harold in whatever mathematics course he needed. He also arranged for a tutored course in Spanish. Thus, by pursuing Alfred's plan, Harold could live at home for the entire 1923-1924 school year. The college credits to be earned would amount to almost the same number of credits he'd earn as a college freshman at PUC. Alfred's ingenious plan was adopted, and Harold, though not entirely pleased with the situation, proceeded accordingly. But, as always, God had arrangements of His own for the young student with the overbearing parents.

Providence also brought another major influence into the 17-year-old's world. George H. Skinner became the sanitarium's new chaplain. He had a son, Lawrence, just a year older than Harold. The two became fast friends, attending Sabbath school classes together and sharing the hidden secrets of their hearts.

Harold told his buddy about the unique, one-year college program his father had devised, and Lawrence decided to adopt the plan for himself. In addition to their classes, both took part-time jobs. Harold washed dishes and sterilized the glassware used by medical students in the Department of Bacteriology. Lawrence became a night clerk at the sanitarium.

The ever-vigilant Shryocks became well acquainted with the Skinner boy and quickly approved of his high ethical and moral standards. "He's a fine, representative, Christian young man," Alfred told Stella. "He's athletic and socially inclined. Did you know that young Skinner earned all his own tuition through academy and his first year of college? That young man has exactly the qualities that our son lacks."

The Shryocks liked Lawrence Skinner so much that they decided to trust him to be Harold's college roommate at PUC during the following academic year. At last! Harold was going to live in the dormitory far from his mother's constant oversight.

In time, some of Lawrence's positive influence did rub off on Harold, helping him face the often harsh realities of adult life. His new roommate proved to be reliable and energetic. With a pleasing personality and a stalwart character, he was exactly the role model Harold needed.

The two best friends enjoyed happy times together, interacting with classmates and taking long Sabbath afternoon hikes through the beautiful hills and green-carpeted valleys surrounding the campus. The Shryocks expected and even hoped that Harold would become homesick. But he didn't. On the contrary, he relished being on his own. Going away to college meant achieving a certain level of freedom—the freedom to make at least minor decisions in his life.

⌒

During the summer of 1925, Harold and his father traveled by train during a memorable, three-week vacation, visiting sites of interest throughout the eastern United States.

The two gawked at the monuments and government buildings around Washington D.C., explored the Woolworth skyscraper and Statue of

Liberty in New York, and rode the city's extensive subway system just to see how far they could go for a dime.

They stopped by the Diston Saw Company and Stetson Hat Company; toured the U.S. Steel plant in Gary, Indiana, for a day, observing the entire operation from the open-hearth furnaces to the rolling mills; and witnessed the manufacture of railroad rails.

In silent amazement, they watched the goings on at the Swift Meat Packing Company, and toured the sprawling Eastman Kodak Company in Rochester, New York. On a swing through Boston, the two adventurers strolled around the nearby historic villages of Lexington and Concord. In Detroit, Michigan, they saw automobiles being put together on the busy, state-of-the-art assembly lines at Ford Motor Company.

Alfred designed the entire trip to provide Harold with an insight into American history and industry. For three weeks, 19-year-old Harold had an entire country for a classroom.

Following the trip, and for the remainder of the summer, Harold lived at home in Loma Linda, working at the CME maintenance shops, where he took inventory of hardware and building supplies. He also played cello in Dr. Floyd Gardner's Loma Linda Orchestra, which on several occasions joined a larger orchestra for concerts in the Redlands Bowl.

One evening, after a concert, the socially shy Harold became bold enough to ask a former PUC classmate, now a secretary at the sanitarium, if he could take her home. She accepted. Several dates followed. Alfred and Stella not only allowed him to pursue a social life, but also permitted him to use the family car in order to accomplish it!

⌒

When Harold returned to PUC for his third and final year of pre-medicine, a combination of circumstances led him to postpone any other romantic activities and focus entirely on his studies.

Since Harold had already taken his required chemistry classes at Loma Linda, Raymond Mortensen, the young chemistry professor, placed him in charge of the students' organic chemistry lab. Here, he maintained the reagents, assigned laboratory equipment, and graded papers.

Harold's course of study included several electives, public speaking one and two, public procedures (parliamentary law), general psychology, child psychology, and printing. Providentially, some of these courses broadened the foundation for Harold's career in education and administration and set the stage for avocations in counseling, writing, and public speaking.

The public speaking courses, taught by Professor Charles E. Weniger, offered much more than the fundamentals of appearing before an audience. Weniger instilled in his students such timeless principles as integrity, humanitarian service, and culture.

During the course in public procedure, Harold's class moved, seconded, and voted to spend a day at the state legislature in Sacramento to witness parliamentary rules in action. This class taught the young student procedures he'd someday use as an administrator at CME.

An assignment in his rhetoric class led to his participation in a formal debate, which included oratory, gesticulation, and even feigned enthusiasm and conviction. He would put these effective techniques to good use years later with real conviction.

During Harold's two years as a premedical student at PUC, he began to overcome some of the social handicaps that had plagued him. He was voted "king" of the men's club, an honor that reassured him he was attaining some peer acceptance. He also became the leader of a young men's prayer group, Sabbath school teacher, and secretary of the Missionary Volunteer Society.

Even though Harold was preparing to become a physician—not an easy course of study by any measure—he was simply following the path of least resistance. His father assured him that he could choose whatever honorable vocation he wanted. At one time he considered becoming a minister. Because he had always enjoyed writing, he also considered journalism. But he received no encouragement to pursue these careers.

Lawrence and Harold discussed their career options at length, but did not resolve them. However, his roommate inadvertently introduced Harold to someone who would profoundly impact his future.

During the summer vacation between Harold's two years at PUC, the business department of CME had employed Lawrence to inventory furniture in the nurses' dormitory on the Los Angeles campus. One particular nursing student caught his attention.

While crawling under a table looking for an inventory number, Lawrence accidentally knocked a lamp onto the floor. Although the lamp didn't break, he felt embarrassed for being so clumsy, especially since the accident took place in plain view of the lovely coed.

"Oh, I'm so sorry," Lawrence gasped as he picked up the shade and returned it to its proper place on the table.

"That's OK," the young woman said with a smile. "You'd think they'd put inventory numbers where they were more easily read. Are . . . are you OK?"

"Me? Oh, I'm fine." The boy brushed himself off, trying to look just a *little* shaken by the experience.

"Well, that lamp could've hit you on the head or something. You could've been hurt."

Lawrence nodded soberly. "Funny, I never thought of taking inventory as a dangerous profession."

The young woman held out her hand, and Lawrence noticed it was filled with a collection of small, round, bright-red fruit. "Have some cherries," she invited. "They'll make you feel better."

Lawrence accepted the gift, happy for something on which to focus his attention rather than his companion's beguiling smile. "Thanks. Uh, I didn't catch your name."

"Daisy," the girl stated as she turned to leave. "Daisy Bagwell. Enjoy the cherries. See you later."

"Yeah. I'll . . . I'll see you. Thanks."

When he returned to PUC the next year, Lawrence mentioned his encounter to Harold and added with some degree of satisfaction that the girl with the cherries was transferring to the School of Nursing at nearby St. Helena Sanitarium and Hospital. "Very convenient," he said.

Over the course of the next year, Lawrence visited Daisy at the sanitarium on several occasions.

In late April of 1926, toward the end of Harold's second school year at PUC and just after he turned 20, a schoolmate, Wilton Thomas, invited him to go on a double blind date. It seemed that Wilton's mother had been a patient at St. Helena Sanitarium and Hospital and had been favorably impressed by two of its student nurses—Hazel Gronemeyer and Daisy Bagwell. She was so impressed that, as a gesture of appreciation, she wanted the two young women to spend a weekend at her home in Berkeley.

Son Wilton, thinking that two nursing students might be a little more than he could handle alone, invited Harold to accompany him for a special weekend at his parents' home. The offer took Harold by surprise. Although he and Wilton lived in the same dormitory, they didn't really know each other very well. They weren't even classmates.

Wilton mentioned that one of the girls joining them to celebrate his mother's recovery was Daisy Bagwell. Harold frowned. Did he dare accept this invitation when it would mean spending a weekend with his very own roommate's friend? Could he do this to the young man whose companionship had meant so much to him?

"When do we leave?" Harold responded with a grin. "Sounds like fun!"

Harold and Daisy had met once before, but Lawrence had made sure that the introduction was brief and to the point. Harold remembered Daisy as being friendly and sociable. But now he'd be escorting her on an actual date . . . sort of.

He immediately wrote to his parents and obtained their institution-required written permission for an off-campus leave. The one person to whom he did not mention the upcoming event was his friend Lawrence.

The weekend adventure at the Thomas home proved to be most pleasant. Wilton's dad, Reed Thomas, part owner of a Berkeley automobile agency, drove the four to the Thomas residence in a shiny new car. Friday evening, the two couples took a sightseeing ride through Berkeley; and, the next day, they attended church and, later, sang songs in the Thomas parlor. Saturday night brought popped corn, sandwiches, and funny stories. For Harold, Sunday came far too soon.

The young man found that he was beginning to truly admire the vivacious 21-year-old Daisy. In his mind, she was unusual—a combination of friendly but not frivolous.

An occasional comment in her conversation indicated that she'd been through some unpleasant experiences as a child and teenager, but it seemed that she'd learned to benefit from those difficulties. She appeared self-confident, but not egotistical, and had a genuine Christian perspective.

Harold decided that he wanted to get to know her better. But how? As a prospective medical student, he'd soon finish his studies at PUC and return to Loma Linda. Daisy had one more year of nurse's training to complete, and then she'd be concerned about passing the state boards. Then there'd be career choices to make.

While she seemed mildly responsive to his desire to cultivate a friendship, they both realized that simple logistics weren't working in their favor.

Word of the weekend excursion spread around campus; when Harold returned to the dormitory, Lawrence was waiting.

"So," he said with a scowl, "now you're taking out my girl. *My* girl! What do you have to say for yourself?"

Harold looked over at his friend. "One weekend isn't going to change the world. Besides, I'm premed, and she's a nursing student. Sit down with our schedules and work out a romance for us, OK? And unless you're hearing something I don't, there are no wedding bells ringing on campus. It was fun, but now it's over."

"Why didn't you tell me about this weekend?" Lawrence pressed.

"I knew you might be upset."

"Might be? Of course, I'd be upset, but not as much as I am now! You're supposed to be my friend, Harold Shryock."

"I *am* your friend. And that's all I am to Daisy, too. We're friends, Lawrence."

His roommate's face relaxed just a little. "You should have told me."

His companion nodded. "Yes, I guess I should have."

In time, he and Lawrence moved back to stable ground, but Harold couldn't help feeling that maybe, just maybe, there could be more to his relationship with Daisy than a fun weekend in Berkeley. He was learning, even at a young age, that the hand of Providence has a way of interfering with young men's dreams and the set-in-stone direction people arrange for their lives. In time, his inner thoughts would prove amazingly accurate.

The team of Shryock and Skinner roomed together for two years. Both were set to graduate on May 16, 1926. But graduation weekend presented yet another minor social quandary.

Harold's growing friendship with Daisy Bagwell was becoming more and more important to him. His parents had planned to visit for the weekend, and he certainly didn't want to ignore them. But he didn't want to ignore Daisy, either.

Sabbath afternoon Harold introduced his parents to Daisy and a classmate at St. Helena Sanitarium. "Very nice girls," Mom and Dad said courteously, before whisking their son away to meet and greet others in the crowd. Little did either of them know what a significant role Daisy would play in their son's life.

Following graduation, Harold returned to Loma Linda and immersed himself in the medical course. Now Harold decided to focus his energies, unreservedly, on academic pursuits. He stopped playing in the orchestra, dropped any attempt to maintain active courtship with anyone, and fantasized about becoming a well-trained specialist in internal medicine.

Still, something about Daisy Bagwell continued to engage his thoughts. There was a mysterious bounce in her personality that set her apart from all the other young women in his life. Although he learned she'd been an orphan, she didn't seem to feel sorry for herself. Even though he had no time to pursue an active courtship with her, he didn't want their budding friendship to wither away. So, he picked up pen and paper and wrote her a letter telling her about his new experiences in medical school. In a few days, a reply showed up in his mailbox. He quickly replied to her reply, and a pattern of correspondence developed.

At first, their letters weren't particularly romantic—just filled with the latest news and information about the general conditions of their work and study. Daisy shared interesting or humorous little stories about her experiences caring for patients, and Harold wrote about the rigors of the medical course. Daisy candidly expressed her faith. In one such letter she wrote about how God had seen her through difficult times as a child and youth, and how she believed that the future was in His hands.

In time, her neatly written, "Sincerely, Daisy" closing changed to a new and exciting expression of affection: "With love."

Even with this inspiring addition to their correspondence, Harold had other, more pressing issues to face. As the son of a medical school professor, he'd not only been exposed to the rigors of studying medicine, but also had heard many stories of students who'd tried and failed to do exactly what he was trying to do. Some barely passed the course.

In college, Harold had carried only a B average. So he tried now to make up in diligence what he lacked in fundamental aptitude. He determined to please his father by leading his class in physiological chemistry, a subject in which he had a particular interest. But he also realized that he was competing against those who were smarter than he, a fact that made his efforts doubly exhausting.

Harold's day started at a regimented 5:30. He applied a lot of self-discipline and studied intensively for many hours every day. And he transformed the Shryock guestroom into his own personal study. The result? His grades climbed. He joined his classmates in philosophizing about the demanding curriculum. "Students ahead of us have made it," they chanted to each other. "We can make it, too!"

In his quest to excel Harold began to neglect exercise and recreation. He hadn't realized yet that every person has a limit of tolerance, beyond which body and brain both rebel. After several months in medical school, he began to experience some mysterious symptoms. He couldn't sleep. He suffered from frequent headaches. He had difficulty concentrating on what he read. His energy, endurance, and ambition dropped to zero.

"Sounds like you might have an intestinal parasitic infection or maybe an endocrine disturbance," his doctor stated, reaching for a notepad. "I'll prescribe some powerful anti-parasite drugs. Should help."

They didn't.

"You might have chronic appendicitis," someone else suggested. Trouble was, nobody knew exactly what chronic appendicitis might be. Dr. Will George, the sanitarium surgeon, hadn't even heard of it, but other physicians pressed him to do an exploratory surgery, during which he removed Harold's perfectly healthy appendix.

Harold's condition continued to decline.

Over the coming months Harold endured many tests, yet his physicians could not determine the cause of his symptoms. No one in Loma Linda had even considered that the young medical student had simply exceeded his endurance. The various remedies they prescribed, including surgery, didn't enable Harold to resume his medical studies; and, after a few months, he was forced to do something he'd never imagined he'd do: he dropped out of medical school.

Fred E. Herzer, M.D., a CME graduate and Glendale pathologist who'd gained some valuable insight into human nature, told the despondent student, "What you need is to engage in some form of pleasant, active recreation—like playing tennis. You have burned yourself out mentally, young man. Learn to take it easy."

As weeks turned into months, Harold began to hope that he'd be able to resume schoolwork by joining the next freshman class. But there was more fear hiding in Harold's heart. Daisy. Why would she want to cultivate a friendship with someone with such a doubtful future? With trembling hands, he wrote to her, pouring out the details of his condition, without holding back the shadows that darkened his future. When he sent the letter, he figured their courtship had ended.

To his utter surprise and amazement, she wrote back. Even though he considered himself an invalid and told her so, Daisy continued to fan the slow-burning flames of their friendship.

Since Alfred usually picked up the mail, he brought something important to Harold's attention. "If you like this girl," he said, dropping the latest letter from her on his desk, "why don't you tell her how to spell your last name?" Daisy had heard Harold's last name but had never seen it in print. So, with a gentle smile lifting the corners of his mouth, he explained to his faraway friend that that the "r" should come before the "y." Shryock.

Now that he was no longer in medical school and couldn't work, Harold had time to write longer letters to his distant pen pal. Daisy responded in kind, her messages always filled with words of encouragement. Her optimism seemed endless. After a year had elapsed, even his comment that he "might not be able to resume the medical course" didn't discourage her.

Because of her sympathetic interest, Harold concluded that Daisy's feelings were truly genuine, and her personal values far from superficial.

Harold's illness gave him time to ponder his destiny. On the one hand, he'd scholastically qualified to attend medical school. On the other, he had no adequate preparation for any career, other than being a physician. What to do? Maybe someday he'd be a teacher, like his father, and avoid the strenuous practice of clinical medicine.

During this time of awful uncertainty, Harold refused to consider courtship. Greatly humbled, he realized that he was not the captain of his own life's voyage. Under the circumstances, the prospect of marriage didn't even cross his mind. First, before anything else, he must stabilize his health, reenter his study of the basic sciences, and get his career back on track.

But, as time slipped by, Harold needed someone in whom to confide. He needed Daisy. Correspondence was great. But how he wished he could sit down and actually *talk* with her, to hear the sound of her voice! He longed to listen to her words, not just read them scrawled on a piece of paper.

She often spoke of trusting God to guide his future, just as He had for her. The young man with the mysterious illness wanted desperately to develop such a trust.

"The most important things in life aren't tied up in professional degrees or popularity," she wrote, "and they certainly aren't measured in dollars and cents."

The woman's words began to eat away at his uncertainties and fears. Her stalwart trust in Divine Power and belief in providential leading brought renewed hope into his existence. He *was* important, he was *valuable;* not for what he could *do,* but for what he *was:* a child of God.

Educational challenges, frustrations, and uncertainties had marked Harold's teen years. But during that time, Providence had been nudging him to develop very specific talents and skills, which would contribute to an unparalleled personal ministry, exceeding anyone's imagination and even his own expectations. Harold's life would become a flesh-and-blood example of just how Providence can use an imperfect vessel for God's glory.

But for now, deep within his pain, one light still shone brightly, offering him hope beyond his darkest day. That light was Daisy.

Chapter 4

Just One Daisy

rovidence couldn't have joined two more distinctly different people. Harold had been sheltered and constantly supervised by dominant parents; Daisy had been orphaned, treated much like an outcast, never indulged or pampered. She learned early to fend for herself.

Born July 15, 1904, Daisy soon became the responsibility of a childless couple. Jim and Jenny Bagwell lived on a pear ranch owned by the Morse Seed Company, three miles from Santa Clara, California.

When the Bagwells decided to adopt, Jim specifically wanted a boy to help him manage the ranch. With this thought in mind, Jenny boarded the train for the 40-mile trip to a Catholic orphanage in San Francisco, eager to find a healthy, strong son.

The nuns who met her simply led her to a large room. "Take your time," they told her, pointing at the collection of bundled infants lying in colorful cribs. "Inspect the babies one by one. Then choose the child who smiles at you and holds up its arms to be held."

It worked. Jenny was immediately drawn to one particular child everyone called "Happy." Just one problem: he was a she. And the baby didn't even have a real name.

"That's not a son!" Jim growled when he was introduced to the newest member of the family. "What good is a girl on a working ranch?"

In spite of the father's hesitancy, the state authorities accepted the Bagwells' application for a probationary adoption; and the couple named the newcomer "Daisy."

Little Daisy soon began collecting happy memories as she grew. She traveled in a buggy, rode horseback, climbed trees, and hunted for eggs.

She especially enjoyed the harvest season, a time when the ranch's team of six big horses pulled wagonloads of pears to the big shed in town, where Father sold the sweet fruit by the bushel

Daisy's mother proved to be a very loving and kind person. In the evenings, Daisy was allowed to brush her mother's long, beautiful, auburn hair. One morning Daisy found her mother standing by the front door, sobbing. The little girl quietly walked up beside her, stood silent for a moment, and then joined in the crying. *If Mother is hurting,* she figured, *I should be hurting, too.*

The reason for Jenny's sorrow became painfully evident a year later when Jim and Jenny divorced, an event that shocked their daughter. Now 10 years old, Daisy had never seen them quarrel.

Jenny, a devout Catholic, gave the financial settlement to the Catholic Church, and then began supporting herself and Daisy by working as a practical nurse. Mother moved from job to job, making it necessary for her growing daughter to attend a variety of schools. When unable to stay with her mother, Daisy would occasionally live in a Catholic convent.

When Daisy was 12, they moved to a new job: caring for an elderly person in the Twin Peaks area of San Francisco. Daisy took a streetcar to school and cared for the smaller children of the family after classes and on weekends.

Then, suddenly, her world came crashing down around her. Her mother—sweet, attentive, loving Jenny—contracted Addison's disease and was hospitalized. Sensing that she wouldn't recover, the young mother instructed Daisy to find her life insurance policy tucked away in a trunk at home, and take the document to her niece, Edna. While searching through legal papers hidden at the bottom of the trunk, the youngster discovered something she'd never suspected. The Bagwells were not her biological parents. She was adopted.

Daisy planned to ask her mother about this new discovery, but when she returned to the hospital, Jenny had become semicomatose. She died the very next day.

At the funeral, Daisy was the only person seated in the mourners' section. Her adoptive father showed up, but remained in the back of the room and made no contact with her. Wealthy relatives who had discovered oil on their farm in Oklahoma sent her a dollar.

Daisy, now cast adrift without a human rudder for guidance, went to live with relatives, 40 miles away, in Mountain View, California. The adults assigned her the care and feeding of two girls, ages 10 and 7, and a 2-year-old boy. Her new family also dumped a large share of the house-keeping chores on her narrow shoulders, and treated her like a hired servant with no time off. Within a year, the family moved to Lone Pine, California, and they told her that they couldn't take her with them. "You should consider making your own way in life by caring for children," they told the 14-year-old.

To help finance their move, the woman of the house borrowed Daisy's $100 U.S. Liberty Bond. She promised to pay it back as soon as the family settled. The family moved. They settled. The struggling young teen waited in vain for repayment.

But the same hand of Providence guiding the development of a boy named Harold also hovered with utmost love over a girl named Daisy. A Seventh-day Adventist neighbor, Pastor A. O. Tait, who was also editor of *Signs of the Times* magazine, took Daisy into his home until a more permanent home could be found for her. Daisy lived with Pastor and Mrs. Tait for two months. In May 1917, Charles and Laura Lake welcomed the twice-orphaned girl into their family for as long as she cared to stay.

Mr. Lake, a cashier at Pacific Press Publishing Association, was a respected member of the Mountain View City Council. An Irishman, he was always full of fun. The Lakes, missionaries who had recently returned from Japan, already had a 7-year-old adopted daughter named Helen. With eager thankfulness, Daisy accepted the invitation to help care for the young girl and manage the housework in exchange for full room and board.

Right from the start the Lakes liked Daisy, and she liked them. Although they never adopted her, the Lakes treated Daisy as if she were their very own daughter. Since her parents' divorce, nothing but uncertainty and insecurity had filled her life. Now she began to feel as if she belonged.

During her high school days, the girl found another Friend: a glorious Friend whom she knew would stay by her forever! While attending a baptismal class at the Lakes' house of worship, she found Jesus and was baptized into the Seventh-day Adventist Church.

Influenced by the memory of her mother's work and devastating illness, and encouraged by her new family, Daisy decided to become a nurse. But her start toward that particular career didn't go so well.

The Lakes helped Daisy move to the White Memorial Hospital in Los Angeles, where she could begin her first year of nursing school. But she became frightened and homesick in this new, fast-paced environment. After three months, she could take it no longer and returned home to work at Pacific Press.

A year later—now a little older, wiser, and more secure with life—she tried again. Success! She finished her first year of nursing.

But homesickness still plagued her. Then, to her great joy, the Lakes helped her transfer to St. Helena Sanitarium and Hospital School of Nursing in the Napa Valley, where she would be *much* closer to home. Life with the Lakes turned her into a woman of refinement and culture. Apparently, her real parents, whoever they were, had passed on to her a good, solid heredity.

⌒

About this same time, Lawrence Skinner—now a ministerial intern in Escondido, California—was living in a rented room at the Wical residence. Because he had taken all of his science prerequisites to become a physician, local church members felt he was perfectly qualified to become a teacher and asked him to instruct four ninth- and tenth-graders. He accepted the challenge and taught classes in the Wical living room each morning and labored for the church during afternoons and some evenings.

Alfred Wical, the older brother of one of his students, came to the young teacher with an invitation he couldn't refuse.

"I'm going to travel up to southern Oregon to visit relatives," he announced. "Want to come along?"

"Sure!" Lawrence responded immediately. Then he paused. "How are we going to get there?"

"In my car, of course."

Lawrence frowned. "Your car? You mean that wreck parked in the driveway?"

"That's not a wreck. It's a finely tuned machine capable of great speeds and a comfortable ride."

"It's a pile of junk!" Lawrence laughed.

Alfred exclaimed. "I'll have you know that I've been tinkering with that Model T Ford for months. It's in fine shape."

His companion scratched his head. "Fine shape? Let's see. It's just a frame with a steering wheel, an engine, four wheels, and a windshield. It has no fenders, no running boards, no doors, and no body, not even a seat."

"Detail, details," the mechanically resourceful Wical said with a wave of his hand. "So do you want to go with me, or not?"

Lawrence thought for a moment. "I've got this friend convalescing out in Loma Linda. Name's Harold. Can he come, too?"

"The more the merrier," came the quick reply.

Harold readily agreed to the trip—if they would drop him off at PUC. "I really want to visit Daisy," he explained.

To accommodate their camping gear, Alfred attached a wooden box to the old Ford's frame. He and Lawrence sat on a cushion laid across the frame.

When the two adventurers arrived in Loma Linda, Harold found that there was no extra seat for a third passenger, so he made himself comfortable on the floor on the passenger's side, legs dangling over the edge of the frame. He sometimes had to raise his feet, especially on gravel roads. Occasionally, he joined the luggage in the wooden box.

Alfred maintained a fast 45 mph, overtaking most other cars on the road. When the contraption rattled past a real vehicle—one that actually had a body—the trio would shout in unison, "More power to you!"

For Lawrence, the whole trip became a joy ride. For Harold, it combined an escape from reality with a much-anticipated opportunity to visit Daisy.

The journey included a week in Yosemite National Park, where the three intrepid explorers set up camp on the far side of the meadow across from Camp Curry. The boys hiked to Glacier Point for a breathtaking view of Yosemite Valley, Yosemite Falls, and Half Dome. After such an arduous trek, they needed a bit of cleaning up. So, for privacy, they hung blankets from trees and dumped pails of ice cold water carried from the nearby river over whoever was bathing at the time.

The three left Yosemite on a Friday in order to spend Sabbath at the Lodi camp meeting. Then Harold caught a ride with friends to PUC, while his traveling companions turned the "T" northward and rattled toward Oregon.

Harold invited himself to stay in the men's dormitory with Wilton Thomas (who was taking a summer school course in organic chemistry).

Then he hiked down Howell Mountain in the direction of St. Helena Sanitarium and Hospital.

As he walked along the pine-bordered road, he wondered what it would be like to see Daisy again. *We haven't seen each other for more than a year. What are her true feelings for me? Does she still care about me? What's going to happen to us?*

Soon after arriving at the hospital, he caught a glimpse of Daisy dressed in the all-white uniform of a graduate nurse. For an instant, Harold's heart forgot to beat. She was beautiful, and her smile of recognition sent his pulse racing. *Yes, she does still care about me!* he thought with great relief.

Their friendship had matured remarkably during their year of separation. The sentiments they had exchanged in letters had done something to make them very much at ease in each other's presence. Both felt as if they belonged.

That evening spent together confirmed their growing admiration for each other. In the days that followed, the five-mile hikes between the college and the hospital posed no problem for the young man. His spirits were high. Harold smiled often to himself, for he knew he was falling in love.

While they made no promises of continued loyalty, it just seemed that loyalty was understood. They discussed future plans openly and freely, and there was an unspoken sentiment that seemed to whisper, "We'll be experiencing our futures together."

But a barrier existed in their expressions of endearment, through which they dared not pass. Harold didn't have a bank account, paying job, or marketable skill. Under the circumstances, the young man felt reluctant in assuring Daisy of his hopes that their friendship would lead to marriage. He had nothing to offer that would keep the woman of his dreams from accepting attentions from other young men.

"I . . . I don't know if I should try to pursue medicine as a career," he confided hesitantly. "I'm just not sure what to do."

Daisy took his hand in hers. "We need to pray about it," she said quietly.

Harold gasped. She had said we. Daisy was placing them—as a unit—in God's hands. She was saying that they, guided by their heavenly Father, would work things out together.

From that moment on, there was no question in his mind—they were sweethearts.

When Harold's traveling companions arrived to pick him up for the return journey to Loma Linda, he noticed that the vehicle had been slightly reconfigured. "We rolled it," Alfred confessed. "Stripped off the windshield like it was made of paper."

"How did it happen?" Harold inquired.

"Well, we were passing this truck on a dusty road when, lo and behold, here comes another car. What were the chances of that happening? So, to avoid the inevitable head-on collision, we turned the "T" hard-left. The ol' girl went over on her right side, spun around, and dug into the ground, throwing us free. Radiator came apart. Windshield shattered. And she got a great new collection of scratches and dents, where there were none before."

Alfred paused and gazed fondly at the Ford. "Gives 'er character, don't you think?"

Then he added, "By the way, Lawrence and I are fine, just in case you're interested. A few bandages and we're as good as new."

"So," Harold said, eyeing the driver, "will it get us to Loma Linda?"

"No problem," Alfred announced. "Except the replacement radiator doesn't have an overflow pipe to channel any escaping hot water and steam from the radiator to the ground. So I've punched a hole in the radiator cap. Sometimes it gushes like a geyser. Amazing sight! You may have to slide over the hood once in a while and put that metal bucket, upside down, over the cap. Be careful. Water's hot, you know, steaming and all. The windshield post on the passenger's side should keep you from falling off. When the radiator stops spurting, you can slide back into the passenger compartment and hang the bucket over the post. We've got it all worked out. Shouldn't be a problem. Oh, and since our windshield is laying in a thousand pieces in the dirt somewhere in northern California, we've bought these terrific driving goggles for eye protection. Can't be too safe, you know."

"Is that all?" Harold asked.

"Well, one of the tires keeps falling off."

"OK," Laurence said with a determined nod. "Let's hit the road!"

By the time the boys arrived in Salinas, California, they'd run out of money. "Not to worry," the ever-resourceful Lawrence announced. "I've got a checking account. We've just got to find someone who'll cash a check."

They located an Adventist family and identified themselves as fellow believers. To make sure that they were who they said they were, the man of the house instructed them to sing a song during family worship.

With their new infusion of cash, they continued home, arriving without further incident.

⌒

The distractions of the trip, combined with the opportunity to visit with his sweetheart, provided a wonderful diversion for Harold. His health improved enough so that he even resumed his studies. Still not robust, he convinced himself that he didn't have to compete for the highest grades in the class.

Risley, now dean of the School of Medicine, remembered that Harold had done well in his chemistry studies with the dietetics students years before. So he made a concession that helped not only the struggling young man but also accommodated the needs of CME.

Harold became a half-time teacher and a half-time student. He taught organic chemistry to dietetics students, the same course he'd taken as a special student four years earlier. No one foresaw that the young medical student had just begun an early apprenticeship for his lifework. This special program provided Harold experience in teaching that ultimately became more valuable to him and his future career in education than the progress he made toward becoming a physician. He enjoyed being a teacher more than he enjoyed being a student. In addition to teaching organic chemistry to dietetics students, he planned and taught a small course in psychology. Unseen, the hand of Providence was preparing Harold to become a counselor.

⌒

At the end of 1927, driving his parents' 1924 Dodge sedan, Harold shared expenses with friends who wanted to visit northern California. Charles Lake arranged for the young suitor to sleep in a boardinghouse at Pacific Press, in Mountain View, and the Lakes welcomed Harold as a guest in their home when he came to visit Daisy a second time. The Lakes treated him as though he belonged in the family.

Mrs. Lake served delightful meals and Mr. Lake chatted with their visitor about his studies and teaching responsibilities at Loma Linda. Harold met Helen, Daisy's little "sister," when the couple caught the girl hiding behind the sofa, listening to what people in love talk about.

Harold deeply appreciated how well the Lakes had cared for his Daisy. They had visited her when she was a student nurse, helped her move several times, and offered guidance for wisely spending the insurance money she inherited from her adoptive mother.

As they looked to the future, there was another potential problem facing the young couple. Out of concern for their only son, the Shryocks had sheltered Harold from many of life's realities. They had known of occasional girlfriends and understood that Daisy was special. They had casually shaken hands with the girl at the time of Harold's graduation from the premedical course at PUC, but hadn't yet had an opportunity to get acquainted.

To meet that challenge head-on, Harold invited Daisy to visit him in Loma Linda. Providentially, the Lakes, wanting to break in a brand-new 1928 Dodge Victory, had arranged to drop in on friends in Glendale. They invited Daisy to accompany them, coordinating the trip with Harold's three-day vacation from class assignments. The timing proved perfect. While the Lakes visited their friends in Glendale, Daisy became a guest of the Shryocks in Loma Linda.

If being the focus of Harold's affections made Daisy feel that she was under his parents' scrutiny, she certainly didn't show it. Harold happily, and with great relief, observed that both his parents received her cordially. So far, so good.

During the next three days, the couple continued to build their relationship. By now, Daisy had been at her new job at Stanford Hospital in Palo Alto for three months. She had been working 12-hour shifts on the men's ward and had interesting stories to tell. Many of the patients were college students, some injured in athletic activities. When one of the patients tried to get familiar with Daisy, she slapped him in the face, much to the amusement of the others. Daisy had spunk. Thereafter, she had no difficulty maintaining her dignity.

The three days passed all too quickly. Harold reluctantly drove Daisy to Glendale to connect with the Lakes. On the way, they summarized the progress they'd made in their growing relationship and confided in each other their interests, hopes, and convictions. Most importantly, they admitted that their love for each other had grown even stronger.

Then Harold remembered the main reason for the visit—to ascertain Daisy's perceptions of his parents.

"So," he said as he steered the car down the highway, "what do you think about my mom and dad?"

Daisy thought for a long moment. When she spoke, her words were carefully selected. "I . . . I do like them and feel they're very sincere Christians. And I really appreciate the fact that they make time each day for family worship. Your dad is certainly dedicated to his career and his students. That's easy to see."

Harold nodded. "And my mother? What do you think of my mother?"

"Well now, you're putting me on the spot," the woman said, hesitating just a little. "You and I have always been forthright with each other, and so I'll have to tell you bluntly my impression. She's a lovely person. A very lovely person."

"But?"

"I gather she's not the proverbial 'motherly' type individual. She treated me kindly, but I did notice a sort of 'this far and no farther' attitude." The young woman thought for a moment. "Maybe I should say that she is dignified or, rather, that she is a professional type person. Yes, that's it. She's very *professional.*"

Harold nodded slowly. His sweetheart's comments may not have been what he wanted to hear, but they were exactly what he'd asked for—an honest appraisal.

Soon, the couple arrived in Glendale and found the Lakes busily loading their car. Harold was ready with an appropriate remark designed to facilitate his romantic endeavors. "Daisy and I have had a wonderful time," he announced, giving his companion a gentle squeeze, "but we've both decided that three months is long enough to wait between visits."

"I agree," Mrs. Lake responded with a smile. "You're welcome to stay at our home anytime you want," she said. Her invitation was like music to Harold's ears!

So began quarterly visits, alternating between Loma Linda and Mountain View, carrying the two love-struck young people ever closer to the decision that both knew would come sooner or later.

Meanwhile, they endured months of separation, miles of travel by train and car, many painful goodbyes, and hours of soul-searching. Then one day in front of the Lakes' home, as the couple sat together in the Shryock family car, Harold pulled from his pocket a new, white-gold engagement watch and held it up for his companion to see. "Daisy Bagwell," he said softly, "will you marry me?"

"Yes," Daisy responded, eyes shimmering with joy.

They quickly planned for wedding bells to ring that summer, 1929. "We can be married here at the Lakes' home," the bride-to-be suggested, "and I'll ask Helen to be my maid of honor."

"I wouldn't want anyone but Lawrence Skinner to stand with me as my best man," Harold said with a broad grin. "Pastor Tait can officiate."

A summer wedding would fit neatly into Harold's educational program too. By July 1929, he'd complete his sophomore year at CME. The newlyweds would have until September to find an apartment and get settled before Harold would begin his junior year in the Los Angeles division of CME. Daisy could work as a registered nurse, perhaps at White Memorial Hospital. It all sounded so absolutely perfect.

But Providence had a different plan in mind—one that would help Harold mature even more and force him to declare emotional independence from his well-meaning parents. It would also demonstrate Daisy's commitment to Harold as a unique individual, a man she knew might never become a doctor.

Chapter 5

Searching for God's Will

Just past the halfway mark of his sophomore year, Harold began to experience some of the mysterious symptoms he'd suffered earlier, though this time they were not as debilitating. The heavy program of teaching and studies he'd endured for 18 months was taking its toll.

When Daisy visited him in Loma Linda at the end of March, the two made a heart-wrenching decision. In order to keep the illness from worsening, Harold would drop out of medical school . . . again.

Even though Harold felt incapacitated by the event, Daisy experienced a strange peace of mind and a sense of security about their future. The medical student had preferred Daisy to other girlfriends because of her personality and commitment to spiritual values. He firmly believed that she'd been providentially guided through a maze of childhood hazards. Her experiences had only strengthened her confidence in God's overruling influence.

Daisy's commitment to spiritual values proved even stronger than Harold's. She declared a loyalty to him that wasn't tied to his becoming a physician. In the face of growing uncertainties, she became aware that, as a registered nurse, she might have to be the breadwinner of their new family, at least temporarily.

When they broke the news to Harold's parents, they also unloaded another bombshell. "We've decided to get married at the end of April," they announced, standing in the Shryock living room. "And, yes, we know that's only four weeks away."

"Impossible!" Stella gasped.

Alfred lifted his hands to try to quell the building storm. "Listen, young people. While we're both thrilled that you've found each other, getting married on such short notice is simply not acceptable. There's so much to do, so much planning, organizing, letting friends and family adjust their schedules for the event. We've got to print the invitations, arrange for—"

"Dad," Harold interrupted. "We're not asking whether we can get married in four weeks. We're *telling you.*"

Alfred and Stella stood openmouthed. They'd been in the habit of giving advice and having it accepted without question. Their child had always submitted to his parents' direction in the interest of obedience and respect. The determination and gentle stubbornness he was now demonstrating was new and very unsettling.

"Well . . ." Alfred said when he found his voice, "where . . . where will you work? How will you support a wife?"

Harold frowned. "We've been thinking a lot about that, and we need some help in finding employment."

Alfred grinned broadly. "I know some Adventists up in Portland, Oregon, who run a bakery, and they just might need a new member for their sales team. It's outdoors, lots of physical labor, just what you need right now. I'll give them a call and see if we can work something out. Interested?"

"Sure. I'm willing to give it a try."

The next day, as Harold took Daisy back to Los Angeles to catch the train, they both felt tremendous emotional relief. Future uncertainties made no difference. They knew the road ahead wouldn't be easy. But, now, they were in control of their own destiny. They could depend on each other. And, best of all, they'd be together sooner, rather than later.

The Lakes and Shryocks willingly cooperated and eagerly participated in the big change in plans. Harold dropped out of medical school classes at the beginning of April and asked to be relieved of his teaching responsibilities, while Daisy gave notice to her employers at Stanford Hospital.

⌒

Harold Shryock and Daisy Bagwell were married at the Lakes' home on Bush Street in Mountain View, California, on April 30, 1929, with A. O. Tait officiating. Helen Lake served as bridesmaid, while Herbert Childs, Jr., a nephew of the Lakes, stood in for Lawrence Skinner, who couldn't get away from work long enough to take part in the happy event. Thirty relatives and close friends gave their approval by attending.

That evening, snugly tucked away in room 210 at the Cardinal Hotel in Palo Alto, Harold and Daisy held their very first family worship as husband and wife. As planned, the two read from the Bible the beautiful words, "Entreat me not to leave thee, or to return from following after thee: for whither thou goest, I will go; and where thou lodgest, I will lodge: thy people shall be my people, and thy God my God" (Ruth 1:16).

As a wedding present, Harold's parents had given them $200 cash and an almost new, four-cylinder 1928 Chevrolet coupe, which Harold conveniently stashed in the parking garage under the Cardinal Hotel. The groom enjoyed handing Daisy the second set of car keys, an act that symbolized the establishment of their first community property. This was "their" car, not "his" car. They named the vehicle "Tuesday Night" in celebration of their first evening together as newlyweds.

The Shryocks' honeymoon trip carried them as far as Vancouver, British Columbia, and included a 30-minute ride on a speedboat named "Wallflower."

Following their honeymoon, the couple rented a place at the Waukeena Apartments, 680 East Couch Street in Portland, Oregon, for $33 per month. Harold took a job driving a truck for the Dixie Bakery. The company, which had recently purchased a small fleet of new Chevrolet trucks for house-to-house deliveries, needed salesmen. So it was that Harold traded his student scrubs and instructor smock for a crisp, white "breadman" uniform.

Selling door-to-door wasn't easy for the ex-medical student. Being an introvert, he recoiled at dealing with so many people each day. But it was just the kind of work he needed: employment six days a week, lots of outdoor exercise, regular hours, and enough money on which to live, with a few dollars to spare.

With a bride to support, the sheltered young man who had spent much of his life under the care and feeding of parents became self-sufficient, and able to fend for himself for the first time. Every day he made decisions with long-lasting consequences that affected not only his own well-being but also that of someone he loved.

The couple quickly learned that the freedoms and new horizons of married life contributed to a blessing for which they'd been praying: Harold's health improved with each passing month.

Harold's venture contrasted sharply with anything he'd done previously. A new interest in making friends gradually replaced his initial anxiety in meeting people. Chatting briefly with each customer, he lost his timidity. Soon he was serving about 200 clients, occasionally finding opportunities to discuss religion.

On one occasion, a customer asked the breadman, "Are you a medical student?" When the answer was yes, the woman reported treating her husband for pleurisy with rags soaked in "terpentyme." She claimed that the liquid was "sure penetratin' stuff." As her husband improved, she stated with relief that he "almost caught ammonia!"

By the end of his first month on the job, Harold had increased his income to a quite respectable $30 per week. Sometimes Daisy drove the truck, and Harold perched on the running board. Not having to open the door to get in and out at each stop saved time, allowing the energetic breadman to contact more customers.

Once, while Harold was busy making a sale to the wife of a young physician, Joey, the customer's little boy, went to the curb to talk with Daisy. When his mother called, Joey replied happily, "I'm out here talking to the breadman lady."

One of Harold's customers ordered a cake two days in advance of her son's birthday. When the big day came, the cake wasn't on Harold's rack at the bakery. To maintain his customer's goodwill, Harold left his route, bought a cake from a rival bakery, had it redecorated according to his customer's wishes at his own establishment, and delivered it right on time. The young mother complimented Harold the next day on what a marvelous-tasting cake he'd delivered. Little did she know that the rich taste likely resulted from its two layers of icing!

Most days life moved smoothly for the happy couple. Harold's income met living expenses with enough left over for an occasional simple luxury. Being married provided new adventures and strong feelings of belonging, which neither had experienced in the past. And symptoms of Harold's illness all but vanished. The strenuous work restored Harold's endurance, and also gave him a new perspective on living. One conclusion became more and more obvious as the months passed. He didn't want to spend the rest of his life selling cakes, cookies, and cream puffs.

The Shryocks struggled with what to do. Should Harold return to medical school? Should they go into business?

Answers came gradually. Being a nurse, Daisy wanted to help people as a personal ministry. Harold's motives were not yet as well defined, but he shared his wife's desire for personal ministry—whether in a hospital or classroom.

He was also motivated by Daisy's persistent, simple faith in him. "If you want to be a doctor or teacher, then that's what you should be," she often told him. "Life is a series of choices. So sit yourself down and figure out what's most important to you, and then choose the best way to make it happen!"

In November, Harold parked the company truck behind the bakery, handed in his breadman uniform, said goodbye to his coworkers, and drove home. Soon thereafter, in high spirits and filled with renewed hope, he and Daisy packed their belongings into Tuesday Night and steered the vehicle south for the long trip back to Loma Linda. Harold had made his choice.

⌒

This time around, he worked part-time as a technician in both the anatomy and chemistry departments, while Daisy served part-time as a registered nurse at the new Loma Linda Sanitarium and Hospital. At the end of May 1930, he completed his sophomore year at CME and continued his technician job throughout the summer. But Harold and Daisy didn't move to Los Angeles for his clinical education; Harold experienced yet another detour.

"Harold Shryock?" the voice on the phone queried.

"Yes?"

"This is Pacific Union College calling. Professor Raymond Mortensen plans to take a one-year, graduate-study sabbatical at Stanford University to complete requirements for his doctoral degree in physical chemistry, and we wonder if you'd consider returning to the college as a relief teacher in organic chemistry. Your chemistry professor there at

CME, Dr. Edward Risley, highly recommended you for the job."

Flattered by the invitation, Harold said he'd talk it over with his wife. But he and Daisy felt it would be unrealistic for him to drop out of medical school again. No, such a move, regardless of being for a good cause, would only prolong establishing his medical career and complicate their financial struggles.

"Thank you, but no thank you," Harold told the representative a few days later. "My wife and I have been pinching pennies long enough, and I'd really like to get through my medical course and on with our lives. So, we're not interested."

PUC wasn't about to give up so easily. A little later, Harold received a call from W. E. Nelson, college president. "Harold, we haven't been able to find anyone to fill this position. We really want you to come join us here on the mountain."

After repeated communications, Harold and Daisy decided to list their conditions for accepting the call. "We require 12 months of salary instead of nine," they said. "And we want to be fully reimbursed for our moving expenses. We must have a home in which to live and a bachelor's degree for Harold. (At that time, Adventist senior colleges granted a bachelor's degree to medical students who had completed two years of premedical and two years of medical study at Loma Linda.)

PUC met every condition.

So, once again, Harold and Daisy packed Tuesday Night to the roofline and hit the road, heading north. Harold admitted that he was looking forward to being a teacher where he'd invested happy years as a student and would enjoy spending more time in the beautiful Napa Valley.

Harold's office was located on the second floor of the new three-story science building for the teaching of physics, chemistry, and biology.

As the replacement teacher, Harold quickly realized that Professor Mortensen had been a favorite with students. He could sense their disappointment as he approached his first class session.

For reasons unclear to everyone, Mortensen's students had nicknamed him "Saul," after the ancient king of Israel. So, in response to the awkward situation facing him that first day, Shryock opened his lecture with a story about the biblical characters Jesse and his son David.

"You recall that Jesse became anxious because he hadn't received

word from his older sons, soldiers in the Israelite army, which was suppos-
edly fighting the Philistines," Harold told the surprised faces in the classroom. "He called David, his younger son, and asked him to go where the
army was camped, check on his brothers, and bring him word again.
When David arrived at the battlefield, he found that all was quiet. The soldiers were idle. 'What's the matter?' he asked.

"His brother's responded, 'Haven't you heard about Goliath?'

"After the brothers told David about Goliath, he taunted them for their
fear. But they responded, 'If you think we are cowards, then why don't you
go out and fight with him?'

"David accepted their challenge: 'Sure I'll go.' So they helped David
put on the king's armor and started him out to meet Goliath. But he soon
came back. And what was it that he said? He said, 'I CAN'T FIGHT IN
SAUL'S ARMOR.'"

Smiles of recognition and understanding spread across the faces dotting
the classroom. From that moment, Harold's students became his buddies.

Even though the young replacement hadn't taken a course in quanti-
tative analysis, he brashly accepted the challenge to teach it. He selected a
textbook for the course and studied harder than most students in his class.

Noticing one night that Harold's office light was on at 10:00, a student
asked for help in working out one of the assigned problems. The teacher
smiled shyly. "Sorry," he said. "I can't help you. I'm afraid I don't know
yet how to work it myself. Ask me again tomorrow morning."

In late September of that year, health problems once again darkened
the Shryock home. But this time, it was Daisy who developed puzzling
symptoms. During a pleasure drive to Pope Valley, she experienced a terrible pain in her side. Two physicians recommended surgery. The next
day, she underwent an emergency appendectomy at St. Helena Sanitarium
and Hospital.

After recovering from her ailing appendix, Daisy learned that she had
another medical condition of a much more joyous nature. The Shyrock
family was about to grow, a bit of news that sent the love-struck couple
into mutual ecstasy.

But apart from his emotional high, Harold realized that his teaching position was serving as a turning point in his life. At long last, he'd discovered a profession that truly satisfied him. As time passed, the substitute teacher began picturing himself more as a prospective teacher than as a prospective physician.

Because Harold had so enjoyed the person-to-person contact with students, he thought of a new angle and wrote a letter to his father. "Why should I complete the medical course if I'm going to enter a career of teaching?" he asked. "Would it not be better for me to work toward a doctor's degree in chemistry?"

Alfred quickly conferred with his friend Dean Risley, who chaired the Department of Chemistry at CME, and tactfully inquired whether Harold might eventually be employed as a teacher at the facility.

Risley responded directly to Harold in a letter. "There are so many diseases that you will be studying in your later years," he wrote, "which would give you a basis for your teaching of chemistry in the medical school. For example, nutritional diseases, thyroid diseases, and endocrine disorders; and, of course, nephritis and other degenerative diseases are very closely allied to chemistry of the body.

"I believe that the completion of medical school and a year of internship would open doors to a career in teaching."

Dilemma solved! After his year at PUC ended, Tuesday Night headed south once again, carrying the Shryock family back to medical school. Harold would become a physician.

Chapter 6

On Becoming a Father

T he unexpected seemed to transform Harold's every step during his early years—from maintenance man, laboratory animal technician, truck driver, and medical student to invalid; then medical student to chemistry teacher, suitor, fiancé, husband, and breadman; and now medical student. For the third time!

But most unexpected—well, not entirely—was to learn that his wife was expecting.

Harold moved into an apartment on Pleasant Avenue in Los Angeles near the White Memorial Hospital, where he'd soon begin his clinical education. Daisy took up temporary residence at his parents' home in Loma Linda, where she could enjoy Stella's constant care until the baby was born.

Soon the word came: "Daisy is in labor!"

Immediately, Harold jumped into Tuesday Night and raced to Loma Linda. But Daisy's labor continued much longer than normal, exhausting both mother-to-be and her worried husband.

All day long, Harold held her hand and offered encouragement as the pains grew more intense. Their physician, Dr. Lyra George, stayed with her all day, then gave her a mild anesthetic to help ease Daisy's discomfort. That evening, the nurses wheeled the exhausted woman into the delivery room, and the ordeal ended with the happy announcement, "It's a girl!"

Patricia Helen arrived on September 14, 1931, in perfect condition; but Daisy's energy was so nearly depleted that her uterus couldn't contract after delivery. As a result, she suffered a massive hemorrhage, becoming semi-conscious, and very close to death. Panic filled the delivery room. The fear of tragedy grew as Daisy hallucinated that she was peacefully floating away in space. The little family's future hung precariously in eternity's balance.

Hospitals of that era weren't equipped to perform rapid blood transfusions. A medical team administered an intravenous glucose solution to replace Daisy's lost body fluids, but it could not restore the loss of blood cells. Being a student physician, Harold knew the consequences all too well. The thought of losing Daisy and rearing a motherless child weighed heavily on his aching shoulders. An obstetrician and surgeon worked heroically as the minutes dragged into hours, each tick of the clock echoing and reechoing up and down the hospital corridors like the peal of a distant funeral bell.

Then, slowly, very slowly, Daisy began to recover. Color crept into her skin. Her breathing became less labored, her heart rate less rapid. She began to recognize where she was and the people surrounding her.

Harold felt a touch on his arm. "Mr. Shryock," a nurse said with a smile, "Don't you want to see your daughter?"

His heart brimming with relief and thankfulness, Harold turned away from Daisy and saw his beautiful, blond baby girl. The new father stood motionless, speechless before the tiny infant lying peacefully in her bassinet.

Daisy continued to improve, slowly returning from her dangerous journey to the precipice.

As soon as his wife was out of danger, Harold returned to Los Angeles, while mother and child remained with the Shryocks in Loma Linda, waiting for Daisy's strength to return.

During this time, a pall fell over the Shryock family. Stella made it known that she was not available to help care for the baby. So Alfred changed diapers and brought Patti to Daisy's bedside for feedings during the night.

This new development served as an indication of things to come. At the time, Harold couldn't fully understand the dynamics of the situation; he later grew to believe that his mother's negative response to her new grandchild reflected painful, unresolved issues in her own life, some dating back to her childhood.

As soon as possible, Harold moved his wife and daughter to his Pleasant Avenue apartment in Los Angeles. Even though weak from her ordeal, Daisy managed to care for Patti and keep house while her husband studied and attended classes.

Harold's one-year absence from medical school proved to be of no consequence to his relationships. His new classmates readily accepted and welcomed him.

He participated in outpatient clinics, made hospital rounds, observed surgery, and delivered babies—sometimes in the humble homes of dispensary patients. The schedule for this curriculum, built on a sequential rotation plan, allowed every student experience in each clinical area.

As a major financial depression spread across the country, the little family soon spent the money they'd saved during his year teaching at PUC. Harold worked during the summer of 1932 as a full-time research assistant and, except for the money he earned, Daisy and Harold were totally dependent on an $85 per month allocation provided by Harold's parents.

The elder Shryocks also paid for Harold's medical school tuition. Their dedication to their son and what he was trying to accomplish with his life moved them to this sacrifice. It was much appreciated.

In early April 1932, Daisy told her husband that their little family was about to grow again. On December 9, 1932, Edwin Forrest arrived, red-faced and loud.

As Harold grappled with the challenges of being a senior medical student, Daisy transitioned from working as a charge- and special-duty nurse to being a full-time homemaker and mother of two.

While classmates looked forward to internships, Harold contemplated a career in education. As a physician, he could combine his two passions: medicine and education.

Harold Shryock graduated from CME on June 18, 1933. The ceremonies took place in the Loma Linda Bowl, an outdoor amphitheater on the north slope of sanitarium hill. He stood number eight in scholastic achievement in his class of 93.

As soon as graduation was over, he was eager to take the next step in his career: an internship in Loma Linda.

Harold, Daisy, and their two little ones took up residence in a modest, two-bedroom house on the south side of Prospect Street, two doors west of Anderson Street. Today, the rear of the property borders the double-drive main entrance to Loma Linda University Medical Center.

Conveniently located, they were only two blocks from both the hospital on the hill and the medical school campus.

Living close to campus, Harold could spend his spare time at home. He constructed a two-room playhouse for Patti from some old shipping crates; and she enjoyed playing housekeeper inside while Eddy, assigned the "wild Indian" role in their make-believe world, prowled around outside.

The new Dr. Shryock spent the first three months of his internship at Patton State Hospital, in nearby Highland. He enjoyed his psychology and psychiatry rotations very much; he even delivered two babies at the psychiatric hospital.

During his internship, Shryock administered anesthesia at Loma Linda Sanitarium and Hospital and assisted in surgery. One day, while on that particular job, he suffered a great shock.

☞

A scream shattered the afternoon stillness at Loma Linda Sanitarium and Hospital as the young Harold Shryock flew, uncontrollably, backward through the air. As his body crashed to the floor, it seemed as though all the events of his life passed through his consciousness.

His youth had been a series of incredible twists and turns, false starts, unexplained illnesses, and agonizing delays. Seven years after entering medical school, he'd *finally* arrived at the threshold of becoming a licensed physician; and he had recently discovered the joys and fulfillment of being a loving husband and proud father.

He had anticipated following in his dad's footsteps, and was preparing for an academic career; and he believed his life to be right on track. Now, lying on a sterile hospital floor, his thighs burned, he looked up into anxious faces.

Hospital personnel helped the young physician to a treatment table in the Hydrotherapy Department next door, and tried to make him comfortable. He rested on the table for a half hour, contemplating his fate and hoping that he'd be able to return that evening to his family.

Earlier, while treating a young girl with a broken arm, Thomas I. Zirkle, M.D., had been using a fluoroscope to visualize the bone, while he manipulated it into place. Following the procedure, Harold stood at the girl's head using the standard ether-drip method to administer anesthesia.

As he leaned forward in the darkened room to monitor the drops falling into the patient's mask, his head accidentally touched the X-ray tube. His thighs were already in contact with the metal frame of the examination table; his movement now closed an electrical circuit. Instantly, a current of high-voltage electricity coursed through his forehead, body, and thighs. Muscles throughout his body contracted fiercely. The strong muscles in his back tightened instantly, throwing him away from the X-ray machine, as the current elicited the involuntarily scream heard throughout the building.

Later, Harold learned that a fatal outcome from such an electric shock depended on the phase of the victim's heart action at the instant the current strikes. Had he made contact with the tube a split second sooner or later, he would have been killed.

☞

During his internship, Harold passed the California State Board examination and became licensed to practice medicine in California, even though the license was not required for *teaching* in a medical school. Still, Shryock chose to qualify, just in case he'd ever want to fall back on this alternative career.

The National Board of Medical Examiners also certified him, an endorsement accepted by many states in lieu of passing the license examination. Harold was determined to provide financial stability for his family.

Becoming a father changed him. He loved it. Fatherhood embraced him with fulfillment and pride, which only a loving parent can fully appreciate. Shouldering the responsibilities of dad, physician, and teacher, convinced him: prayer and spirituality were even more important to his career than knowledge and experience. Providence had always been there through his youth—nudging, pointing, directing. And now, standing at the start of his new life, he felt confident that, come what may, the same Power would stand by him as he walked the uncertain paths of his future.

He was right, in more ways than he could imagine.

Chapter 7

Programmed to Teach

arold hoped to launch his teaching career at CME. Toward the end of his internship the faculty wage was boosted to $28 per week—less than the $30 per week Harold had earned as a breadman. He toyed with the idea of building a financial foundation for his family by working at the state hospital for two or three years, before joining the CME team; but Daisy seemed perfectly willing to stay the course.

Harold's first position at CME, instructor of hydrotherapy, enabled him to make friends with all the new students. Guy R. Kaufman, a highly respected nurse, taught practical aspects of the water-based therapy program. As an introduction to his faculty appointment, Harold observed, lectured, and graded tests for Guy.

In his first class of students sat an imposing (6-feet 4-inches tall) artist named Joseph Mossberger. Years before, as a college student, Mossberger had tried to be a miner. Bad idea. Low ceilings!

Instead, he found a job retouching negatives for a photographer. There, in the quiet solitude of the photographic lab, his true talents began to shine. His hands were steady, his brushstrokes carefully controlled. He very quickly discovered that he could not only touch up the creativity of others, he could also create art himself.

One job led to another. Finally, he became a full-fledged artist, opening an industrial art business in Chicago. Now he was looking for even greater challenges.

Harold was fascinated. In the medical world, especially in education, some things simply can't be photographed. Maybe images of them could be *painted*. Such a skill would be invaluable to the educational process, allowing students to study detailed illustrations of the anatomy, even those observed only through a microscope.

When Harold shared his idea with his dad, the man grew excited. Over time, Joseph Mossberger and Alfred Shryock became good friends, and the elder Shryock hired him to illustrate human embryology in watercolor. Mossberger eventually created more than 100 unusual and stunning anatomical drawings for the Department of Anatomy. And his beautiful, airbrushed paintings continue to impress and inspire.

☞

Because members of the CME faculty wore several hats, Harold also began assisting in anatomy, histology, and chemistry.

His father, now age 63, had been teaching microscopic anatomy for 24 years, and he needed to train a successor. Harold assumed that he'd eventually teach chemistry; but, under the circumstances, Dean Risley agreed Harold should join his father, rather than becoming the third man in the Department of Chemistry.

Blessed by their rich relationship, both father and son welcomed the prospect. Harold knew that while he was developing competence, his father would be helpful and patient. He admired his dad as a Christian gentleman, and believed him to be scrupulously honest. Harold wanted to be his father's assistant and automatically anticipated succeeding him. Therefore, courses in histology and embryology became primary interests as he launched his teaching career.

From time to time, Alfred allowed his son to do things he probably wouldn't have permitted others to do. Harold had gained much experience dealing with students, but his lecturing skills needed work. So he was assigned the job of running the projector while Alfred gave presentations, allowing Harold to observe his father's impressive presentation techniques.

Alfred trusted Harold to write essay questions, grade papers, and record student performances. Harold also helped develop equipment to project photographic enlargements of tissue sections to illustrate his father's lectures. During laboratory sessions he circulated among the students and helped them find answers to their questions.

☞

In 1936, about the time Harold's apprenticeship was nearing "gradua-tion," the Shryocks' landlord decided to sell the house they were renting on Prospect Street. This would mean a move. But to where?

Steven Hare, chaplain at Loma Linda Sanitarium and Hospital, offered to sell the Shryocks a lot—some land he owned on North San Bernardino Street (now Campus Street) for $600. Understanding that the Shryocks had no money with which to build a house, he offered to advance them $3,000, at 5 percent interest, with a $1,000 down payment.

When Dean Risley heard about the offer, he appealed to the alumni association, requesting money for the down payment. Eventually, half of the $1,000 came from Risley's efforts and the other half from Harold's par-ents. Harold and Daisy prepared to build their very first home.

Before long, a wooden frame rose over the foundation and, within a few months, the house stood completed, ready to accept the excited fam-ily. It included 1,200 square feet of floor space, plus a half basement, two-car garage, wood stove in the living room, and cement driveway. Total cost: $3,632. Payments: $25 per month.

On moving day, Harold attached roller skates to the bottom of Patti's playhouse and towed it behind his car, west on Prospect Avenue, to their new residence at 115 North San Bernardino Street. The little house rolled slowly through the area that would someday become a breezeway under the outpatient wing at the student entrance of Loma Linda University Medical Center. Patti enjoyed telling everyone that her playhouse roller-skated to its new location.

The property provided room for a vegetable and flower garden. On cold, winter mornings, Eddy stayed in his warm bed until he heard his dad crumpling newspapers, a sure sign that a warm fire would soon be crack-ling in the woodstove, which made getting up much more tolerable.

When Harold went to repay the $500 loan, he discovered that the alumni association had no record of such a transaction on his behalf. What he thought was a loan turned out to be an outright gift from Benton N. Colver, M.D. (AMMC: 1904), a close personal friend of Dean Risley.

In consideration for his years of faithful service to CME, Alfred and Stella Shryock canceled all his indebtedness to them as well.

Although Harold and Daisy were devoted to CME, one day Harold ridiculed his dad for having lived such a self-sacrificing life in Loma Linda. "You left a successful practice of medicine in Seattle and came down here to live like paupers," he told him. "Look at some of your former students. They operate very lucrative practices and live in luxury!"

Alfred thought for a moment, then said, "Harold, you're right. We did sacrifice a lot to be here, to be a part of this institution. But anytime I get to wondering if it was worth it, I just have to think of Elmer Coulston."

Elmer F. Coulston, M.D., was one of Alfred's former students. He married a nurse and accepted a mission appointment. In June 1930, just as he completed his internship and was planning to leave for China, he wrote in the school's newsletter, The Medical Evangelist, "Whatever sacrifice is necessary, I shall willingly make for my Master."

Elmer built a humble practice of medicine and surgery in Kalgan, China. All went well until one day he contracted diphtheria from one of his patients and was confined to bed. When a native woman with an acute need for surgery was brought into his little hospital, the physician stumbled out of his sick bed and performed the operation. The procedure saved the woman's life, but cost Elmer his own. He'd practiced medicine for only four years.

A memorial service was held at the North China Sanitarium. The assistant to Governor She Chi Chiu Jen sent a banner that read, "East and West Unite in Mourning."

The townspeople, so touched by the man's amazing Christian love and devotion, raised a crude stone monument in his honor. "Elmer's life wasn't reflected in the gleam of shiny new cars, the windows of tall, handsome houses, or the shimmer of swimming pools or expensive tableware," Alfred explained to Harold. "His devotion was recorded in stone and placed in the ground by the hands of people who, for the first time, witnessed God's love in action."

Deep inside, Harold Shryock hid his fair share of selfish ambition. Fortunately, Daisy placed a higher priority on unselfish service than on material luxuries. It would have seemed natural for the couple to follow the course of most medical school graduates and seek financial security. After all, with two babies and years of struggle while attending medical school during the Great Depression, gaining wealth would seem almost expected.

But their commitment to CME required a whole new set of devotions, a whole new way of looking at the value of life on this earth. Their self-worth, they decided, would not be determined by their financial situation. Not now. Not ever.

Daisy was happy with what they had and needed little else. If she had longed for material comforts, it would have been easy and natural for Harold to comply in an effort to make her happy. But years before, both Harold and Daisy had decided the simple life of a Christian teacher would be their one and only reward until Jesus came.

⁀

Harold's professional relationship with his father proved energizing, even inspirational. Alfred had worked hard to attain a high degree of expertise in the subjects he taught, and he broadened his knowledge base through continuing education at other institutions.

The CME faculty and administration recognized that the school's on-going accreditation depended on developing programs of scientific research. CME's team of educators drew eagerly, but passively, from the general fund of medical knowledge contributed by the research and experience of others for what they needed to know. Having no faculty engaged in basic research was perceived as a deficiency.

Harold felt a growing need for additional education. Gaining advanced degrees not only would help him carry his fair share of the teaching load but also prepare him to engage in much-needed scientific exploration. So, with his father's blessing, he enrolled as a graduate student at the University of Southern California. Bruce Harrison, Ph.D., Harold's major professor and chair of the Department of Zoology, was favorably inclined toward him because Roger W. Barnes, M.D. (CME: 1922), had recently done very well in graduate studies under his direction. (Dr. Roger Barnes became the grandfather and namesake of Roger Hadley, M.D., present dean of the Loma Linda University School of Medicine.) Harold happily slipped in on the good reputation that Barnes had established. Even Harold's firm belief in Creation didn't pose a problem for Harrison, since the professor also belonged to a Protestant denomination.

In 1939, Harold graduated from USC with a Master of Arts degree in zoology and a minor in psychology, further contributing to his knowledge of the human brain. "I want to know what takes place when a person *thinks,"* he told his professors.

To become better informed on the subject, he'd volunteered, as a freshman and sophomore medical student, to teach the short course in psychology to the dietetics students. Now, with advanced education under his scrubs, he'd be in a better position to teach, counsel, administer, and write on the subject.

When Harold's interest in how the brain works became known to his CME colleagues, Walter E. Macpherson, M.D. (CME: 1924), dean of the Loma Linda division, asked him to develop a course in "psychobiology" for freshman medical students. Harold blinked. "What's that?" he asked.

"Psychobiology, a term coined by Adolf Meyer, the well-known psychiatrist," Macpherson explained, "describes an introduction to psychiatry with emphasis on personality as it relates to physician/patient relationships. It's a course currently being developed in other schools of medicine."

"Is there a textbook?"

"No. No textbook. But you could build on your own professional interest and background in the subject. You can study scientific literature and then write your own. So, would you be interested in developing such a course for CME?"

"Sure," came the confident reply.

Even Daisy and the children got into the act, helping turn the mimeograph machine by hand as they printed copies of Harold's brand-new, smartly written, 100-page syllabus. The children collated the pages and earned three cents per page. Sales of the syllabus through the CME bookstore added a few (much needed) dollars to Shryock's meager income.

Harold proudly opened the doors of his new 15-lecture psychobiology course. As he stood before the class, he began each presentation with what he labeled a unique feature: the class "theme song." He would clear his throat and recite in a clear, strong voice: *"It is quite as important to know what kind of patient the disease has got as to know what kind of disease the patient has got."*

After two or three lectures students began chiming in. By the last session, the chorus of voices was almost deafening.

Shryock's lectures presented simple principles of human relationships, with real-life illustrations—examples he'd gleaned from many different sources. He taught the popular course for 15 years until CME merged it with an introductory course in psychiatry. "This course," according to George T. Harding IV, M.D. (one of Harold's former students, a professor and former Department of Psychiatry chair), "broadened the horizons of most students and contributed to their ability to treat the whole person."

Amazingly, the young man who'd dropped out of medical school for two years because of mental and physical exhaustion was now able to keep pace with his ever-increasing responsibilities. Looking back on those years and marveling at all that had taken place, Harold told friends, "I believe, humbly, that Providence is directing my life and providing the necessary endurance. Also, I now have the undivided loyalty and cooperation of my wife, Daisy, who shares my belief that we are in the place the Lord wants us to fill."

But God wasn't finished yet. He had many more "places" already in the making.

Chapter 8

Responsibilities Increase

acpherson tapped lightly on Harold's office door. "Dr.
Shryock, may I speak with you a moment?"

The teacher looked up from the pile of papers he was
grading. "Certainly. Come in."

Macpherson made himself comfortable in a chair by the
window. He sat for a long moment staring at his coworker. Harold's eye-
brows rose slightly. "May . . . may I help you, Dr. Macpherson?" he asked.

The visitor smiled. "You need more to do."

Harold laughed. "Yeah, I was wondering how to fill up all my free time."

Macpherson chuckled, knowing full well that his friend was already
buried with responsibilities. "As you may have heard," he said with a sigh,
"the Council on Medical Education has expressed displeasure with the way
neuroanatomy is being taught here at CME. Cyril [B. Courville, M.D.,
CME: 1925] is a very gifted and skilled teacher and has taught the class successfully. The quality of his teaching is not the issue. It's timing. In order
to accommodate Courville's professional opportunities at Los Angeles
County General Hospital, neuroanatomy is being taught during the summer between the second and third years of medical school."

Harold lifted his hand. "I thought Courville liked this arrangement.
He doesn't have to travel back and forth to Loma Linda, and ends up
teaching his clinical courses in neurology to the same students who took
his summer course."

"That's true," Macpherson stated with a nod. "But even though you
and I know there's a perfectly sound sequential relationship between neuroanatomy and neurology, the accrediting survey committee is criticizing
the fact that neuroanatomy, which is an elementary, fundamental study, is

not being taught in Loma Linda as part of the *first*-year anatomy course. The committee's recommendations must be followed."

Both sat in silence for a moment, trying to see the situation from the committee's standpoint. Finally, the visitor spoke again. "So, my friend, we were wondering if you'd agree to teach that class. I know it would mean more work and more responsibilities, but everyone is in agreement that you'd be the perfect choice—seeing as you hardly ever have anything to do around here."

Harold grinned broadly. The proposal, coming as an out-of-the-blue surprise, overwhelmed yet thrilled him. Neuroanatomy, one of the most difficult courses in the medical curriculum, was his favorite subject.

"Will you do it?" The question carried a tone of urgency and insistence.

Harold stood and extended his hand. "Consider it done. I'm your man."

With Macpherson's support, the new instructor audited Courville's course during the summer of 1936. Feeling the need for a broader understanding of the structure and functions of the nervous system and to enhance his credentials, Shryock enrolled in a six-week elective course at Harvard University. Neuroanatomy and Neurophysiology required each student to build a scale model of the brainstem and brain.

Harold told the staff at CME that he was very impressed with the advantages of studying the structure (anatomy) and function (physiology) of the nervous system *together,* not separately. In his subsequent teaching of neuroanatomy, he found that showing his students the correlation between structure and function enabled them to learn each more quickly and in greater depth.

Even though inexperienced in teaching neuroanatomy, Harold sincerely tried to perpetuate the highly acclaimed Courville tradition. He worked to develop a course so effective that even Courville himself would be impressed. He divided his "neuro" classes into four lab sections. As the lone instructor, this arrangement allowed him to work intimately with small groups, looking over their shoulders to see whether each student fully understood the assignments.

Student cooperation rewarded Shryock's long hours. He designed his course to be so comprehensive that when students began their junior year, they'd be fully prepared for Courville's class in clinical neurology.

Harold's penchant for uniqueness prompted him to introduce yet another class "theme song," spoken without explanation, at the beginning of each neuroanatomy lecture. He said, *"The secret of success in this course is for the student to adopt and rigidly follow a program of systematic study, being careful at the beginning of each study period to glance backward far enough to sharpen all dull memories."*

Harold didn't ask or suggest that students recite his words, much less learn them. But, as before, the class soon started repeating the words with him in chorus. Years later, former students could still "sing" his neuroanatomy "theme song," much to Harold's surprise and amusement.

Shryock understood that becoming an effective and successful physician took more than knowledge of facts and procedures. As important as those were, he felt that another aspect of caring for the ill needed attention. Harold desired to prepare himself and his students for *real-world* patient-physician interaction.

Because he was unable to bring patients to his basic sciences class, he traveled to Los Angeles every Thursday afternoon to attend Courville's Neuropathological Conference, where he and students displayed and examined brain specimens from recent autopsies. That same evening, he attended the Los Angeles Neurological Society meetings at Los Angeles County General Hospital, where neurologists and neurosurgeons from throughout Southern California gathered to discuss three or four current cases.

After studying any surgery or pathology reports, Harold closely monitored the observations of resident physicians and responses of the neurologists. Then he added these actual case histories to his files. When appropriate, he reviewed them before his class to illustrate their assignments. In this way, he presented a variety of brain lesions and current neurosurgical procedures to help student physicians equate their daily assignments to real-life clinical medicine.

Shryock successfully convinced pathology residents at Los Angeles County General Hospital to save "normal" brain specimens for his students to dissect in Loma Linda. He did everything in his power to stimulate and encourage students, making liberal use of teaching aids—including models. Students and even visiting anatomists greatly admired Shryock's colorful and very effective teaching aids.

Harold knew that careful preparation enabled him to do his best work. Patti and Ed remember their dad coming home at the end of the day, changing into his work clothes, and tending his flowers, yard, and garden. After eating dinner with his family, he would shower and return to his office, where he carefully updated and practiced his lectures for the next day. Staying until he was satisfied that he was well prepared, he often didn't return home until after midnight.

Harold's lectures grew comprehensive and eloquent, and he often demonstrated his important points by drawing on the blackboard with both hands simultaneously, a skill he learned from Courville.

Shryock's syllabus included all the items covered in his lectures. He increased his own knowledge by incorporating information from available textbooks, as well as from current scientific literature. The one-semester course in neuroanatomy lasted only 18 weeks per year, but Shryock's attendance at the weekly neurology clinics in Los Angeles continued year-round.

In November 1942, as World War II raged across the European and Pacific theaters, Harold visited Kenneth Abbott, M.D. (CME: 1936), one of his former PUC students who'd become a neurosurgery fellow at Mayo Clinic in Rochester, Minnesota. Abbott introduced Harold to Dr. Alfred Adson, a leading neurosurgeon, explaining that Harold taught neuroanatomy at CME and wanted to observe what took place in the specialties of neurology and neurosurgery. This valuable contact provided meaningful additions to Shryock's case histories and taught him important lessons in dealing with people with neurological disorders. Adson's tact and diplomacy with patients and their relatives only amplified his reputation for excellent clinical judgment and surgical skill.

In one particularly difficult case, Adson looked up into the amphitheater and spotted Harold sitting among the doctors and medical students. "Dr. Shryock," he called, "I want you to come down here and see these structures that I've exposed." Harold wasted no time in responding, his eager appearance causing the nurses at the operating table to fly into a panic in their efforts to drape him properly in sterile garments.

What he saw caused his heart to skip a beat. There, open before him in plain view within a still-living patient, were the very structures about which he'd been teaching freshman students.

☜

Teaching offered occasional challenges, including what to do about tardy students. Harold developed a unique way of motivating his charges to be on time. He'd stop his lecture, quietly watching the tardy student walk to his or her seat. The interruption so annoyed fellow students that they'd chant, "Sit, sit, sit."

When the guilty party sat down, Harold would continue. Such orchestrated peer pressure effectively motivated many of CME's future physicians to avoid tardiness.

Making his basic science classes interesting challenged him as well. Over the years, some students had been tempted to consider the basic sciences as a "necessary evil"—something to be endured until they could begin seeing real patients. Shryock wanted to impress on them that neuroanatomy was vital to their eventual success as a practicing physician. "An acquaintance with the nervous system," he told them, "could prove essential to your diagnosis and treatment of many different kinds of diseases."

As a conscientious teacher-investigator, Shryock subscribed to the principle that the teacher must "publish" or imprint vital information in the minds of his students, information that would be ready at a moment's notice when a patient's life hung in the balance.

As a result, Harold utilized several kinds of examinations to determine his students' comprehension. He designed small examinations to help students from procrastinating and convey what to look for in the final exam. Then he held 15- to 20-minute oral tests, usually administered to one student at a time at the end of the course. Testing a large class would take several hours. Harold designed this particular exam for two purposes: to test student knowledge and reveal areas he needed to emphasize.

Harold's final exams carried the most weight and determined each student's scholastic class standing.

In 1937 Shryock looked for ways to enliven the study of the structure of the nervous system. Illustrations in neuroanatomy textbooks consisted of basic details of the nervous system, plus line drawings. Taking a cue from his father, he envisioned large, three-dimensional anatomical models with color-coded components to help medical students learn and appreciate the intricate details of the brain.

To accomplish this, he'd need to find a fundamentally ingenious and skillful artist who also just happened to be brilliant.

Where did he find such a person? Right there in his neuroanatomy class. Robert Knighton, a graduate of PUC, was a neat and diligent A student who cleverly discovered ways to accomplish the impossible.

His representation of the human central nervous system, which students dubbed, "The White Elephant," attracted the most attention. In amazing detail, and in unique three-dimensional perspective, it showed the nerve tracts as they originated, traversed, and terminated in various locations in the spinal cord, brain stem, and cortex.

While Robert made teaching models, Shryock perceived that his star student had an aptitude for more important endeavors. To demonstrate his appreciation, Shryock invited Knighton to accompany him to the Thursday evening Los Angeles Neurological Society meetings at Los Angeles County General Hospital.

Robert S. Knighton, M.D. (CME: 1943), a soft-spoken perfectionist, later became a highly renowned neurosurgeon at Henry Ford Hospital in Detroit, Michigan. His surgical skills would one day have a major impact on Harold Shryock' s family.

⌒

CME continued to operate under the handicap of meager finances, primitive equipment, and almost nonexistent research assistants. Ongoing and heavy teaching responsibilities prevented the professional staff from engaging in much-needed research. Shryock firmly believed that an ongoing research program would stimulate the faculty, improve the quality of teaching, and increase the students' appreciation for their school. Maintaining the status quo would lead to an inferior medical education.

Thanks to private funding, other institutions that were scientifically productive were beginning to overshadow his beloved CME.

Wanting to help correct this perceived weakness, Shryock tried in his own way to conduct basic research projects. His efforts resulted in 15 published scientific articles in the areas of cytogenesis (the formation of cells) and congenital anomalies of the nervous system. Coauthors included CME alumni, a resident physician at Los Angeles County General Hospital, and CME faculty colleagues.

In several instances, Shryock involved students and proudly published their names as participants.

Some of the articles reported congenital anomalies researched in the CME Department of Anatomy, including an illustrated description of methods developed at Loma Linda to help medical students visualize the internal features of the human brain. The American Association of Anatomists admitted Harold Shryock to membership on the strength of that article alone.

$\Longrightarrow$

Meanwhile, back on North San Bernardino Street, Daisy shouldered the responsibilities of the home front almost single-handedly. She felt that Patti and Eddy, now 8 and 6, deserved more of a good father's influence than they'd been receiving.

A very conscientious and sincere Christian as well as devoted wife and mother, Daisy remained perfectly loyal to the convictions she'd formed years before, when she became a member of the Seventh-day Adventist Church. Now she desired to provide for her children the life-enriching advantages of a consistent Christian home.

While Harold readily agreed, he didn't know where to draw the line, between being an attentive father and carrying on his career in education, which he and Daisy felt had been providentially planned.

Unfortunately, circumstances didn't allow Harold to reduce his professional responsibilities. In 1940, after Harold's very enjoyable first six years on the CME faculty, Alfred suffered a debilitating stroke that prevented him from lecturing. Without hesitation, Harold took over his father's classes in histology and embryology, in addition to his own responsibilities in neuroanatomy.

Harold tried to get involved with his children whenever possible. In the summertime, when Eddy got bored, Harold found things in the anatomy department for him to do. The job Eddy liked best was running the elevator up and down, from the basement where human remains were stored, to the laboratory upstairs where freshman medical students performed dissections.

As Harold and his career matured, it became clear that his commitment to CME was solid. But his career impacted their family life so much that Daisy became concerned.

Chapter 9

On Becoming a Dean

A great sadness darkened the hallways of CME during the summer of 1943. Edward H. Risley, the man who'd helped steer the course of the institution for so many years, died suddenly.

The board of trustees named Newton Evans, M.D., an experienced administrator, to replace Risley as dean. But it would be a year before Evans could be released from his responsibilities at Los Angeles County General Hospital. So President Macpherson asked Harold to become acting dean of the Loma Linda division, until Evans became available. "With the Lord's help," Harold said, "I'll do my best."

Macpherson gratefully coached Shryock on his new duties.

Carrying a full teaching load, Harold gave up his research projects; and, while shouldering his new responsibilities, he streamlined his activities as much as possible in order to continue teaching his courses in neuroanatomy and psychobiology. The simple organizational structure of the institution increased the burden pressing down on Harold's administrative shoulders. The dean's office coordinated almost everything outside of the actual teaching of classes. In his new capacity, Harold dealt with the news media, handled student discipline, arranged for semiweekly chapel programs, and became a member of CME's board of trustees.

Monthly board meetings alternated between Loma Linda and Los Angeles. Shryock supervised the registrar's office and the admission of freshman medical students, presided over the faculty council every two weeks, consulted with each department to prepare the annual budget, and balanced ongoing and projected departmental needs, using the meager financial resources available. Correspondence also consumed many hours of his time.

Because of the demands of his new responsibilities, Harold couldn't keep up with the pile of scientific literature trying to overwhelm his desk-top. It wasn't very long before the fledgling administrator learned that he did not like being dean.

⌒

World War II further complicated Harold's life. At the beginning of his tenure in the dean's office, the United States War Department virtually commandeered America's medical schools, including CME. This takeover partially ensured that draft dodgers would not use their professed interest in the study of medicine to postpone their induction into military service. It also increased the number of physicians available for the war effort.

To assure a steady stream of young physicians ready to serve as medi-cal officers in the United States military, the War Department imple-mented its "accelerated program," beginning July 1, 1943. In the interest of national security, CME cooperated.

One complication required divine intervention. The military assumed authority for placing medical school applicants. They also announced that the names of all medical student hopefuls would be chosen at random in Washington, D.C. This process would bring to CME a diverse student population, many largely out of harmony with the tobacco-, alcohol-, and meat-free campus. It would also introduce students who were totally un-acquainted with the school's religious ideals to the medical facility. It was definitely a time of crisis!

The CME board of trustees quickly sent President Macpherson to Washington, D.C., where the military shunted him from one colonel to another, ending with a Colonel White. As Macpherson presented CME's problem to the officer, the colonel received a communiqué announcing his promotion to the rank of general. Elevated and aglow with goodwill, White promised to keep Loma Linda in mind as he drafted future details of the program. Providentially, CME became the only school of medicine in America allowed to choose its own students, starting with those who were about to be assigned to other schools.

Drastic changes swept over the campus, too. The Army ordered CME to increase its freshman class size from 75 to 100 per year and told the school it must launch a new class every nine months, instead of 12. It also ordered the reduction of the medical school curriculum from four years to three and eliminated all vacations. Freshman classes started on July 1, rather than in September.

In the past, arriving students were civilians with no military responsibilities. Most male members of this class were of military age, but had been deferred from active military service as a courtesy by their respective draft boards. Now the new regulations required them to sign up with the United States military immediately.

In the summer of 1943, the CME board of trustees approved the installation of Army Specialized Training Program Number 3934 on both the Loma Linda and Los Angeles campuses. On September 15, CME welcomed ASTP 3934 to the facility, complete with military headquarters in the new men's dormitory. As a symbol of coauthority, the major in charge of the military cadre of two lieutenants and four enlisted men requested to have his office next to Dean Shryock's.

The relationship was supposed to be one of host and guest—CME being the host, the new army unit being the guest. At times, however, the guest tried to play host. The first Army officer incorrectly assumed that *all* campus facilities were under his command. He forced compromises in the scheduling of classes and laboratory sessions in order to accommodate military instructions, marching, and gas mask drills.

Several months later, a businessman from the Army reserves replaced that officer and the new commandant was much more cooperative, honoring the religious convictions he encountered.

CME continued to observe Saturday as a day of freedom from classes *and* military activities on campus. The military honored CME's preference for a vegetarian diet, and the cadre of military officers complied with CME's prohibitions against the use of alcoholic beverages and tobacco. From then on, occasions of disputed authority were few and far between.

At the conclusion of their medical training at CME, the new physicians became commissioned officers and stood available for military service.

Some perks definitely came with having the United States military parked on CME's premises—extra, unexpected financial benefits that proved stimulating to both student and institution. Uniforms and tuition came courtesy of Uncle Sam. Students pocketed a stipend that was greater than the wages of an unskilled laborer. Wives and children bought discounted goods at the PX, located in the men's dorm, and could look forward to future veteran's benefits. After one scholar bought a car, the faculty council noted that the students were faring better financially than their teachers.

However, the new accelerated program further complicated the acting dean's life. The nine-month cycle didn't match the 12-month cycle of Adventist senior colleges, where most premedical students were taking prerequisite courses. Prospects in those schools sometimes had to wait several months before entering CME's next freshman class. During this period, some local Selective Service System boards attempted to induct these young people into the military, even though they'd already been admitted to medical school at CME. Harold endlessly negotiated with local and states boards and even the National Selective Service System office in Washington, D.C., trying to obtain temporary deferments for prospective students.

Shryock's one-year experience in the dean's office made crystal clear his preference for being in the classroom.

⌒

Harold happily returned to full-time teaching in the summer of 1944, when Evans moved to Loma Linda and became dean. But, within a year, Evans died unexpectedly. Once again, Macpherson appeared at Harold's office door asking him to become full-time dean of the Loma Linda campus.

When the new appointee returned home from work that evening, Daisy was standing at the kitchen sink preparing supper. He kissed her and remarked, "Congratulations, you've just been kissed by CME's new dean."

Tears filled Daisy's eyes, but they weren't tears of joy. "Harold," she said in a voice far from its usual warmth, "you know that administrative work deprives the children and me of your time and companionship. You have become a stranger in your own home."

Harold nodded. "But, didn't we give first priority to what you and I believed was the Lord's intention for us? That's why we're here at CME, instead of trying to be comfortable in a lucrative practice."

"I don't think God wants us to sacrifice our family in order to accomplish His work," Daisy countered.

In spite of Daisy's objections, Harold functioned in the dean's office in one capacity or another for a total of nine years, serving as dean of the Loma Linda division, associate dean, and finally dean. As before, he became a member of the board of trustees, where fellow administrators knew him to be a fair and reasonable man, a contributor to committee discussions, and a skillful negotiator. For several years he advised the freshman class in the School of Medicine.

As expected, Harold routinely worked long hours. Often he arose as early as 4:00 a.m. and didn't return home until 10:00 or 11:00 at night, or even later. "About the only time I get to see Dad is around the meal table or on the weekends," Eddy, now almost a teenager, complained to his mother. "Even when he's clipping the hedge, his mind is thinking about some problem at work. It's like he's here, but he's not."

"I know," was all Daisy could say.

When World War II ended, a feeling of euphoria swept the country. In spite of their joy, the faculty, staff, and students of CME found themselves missing the ASTP 3934 cadre of military officers who'd been their constant companions for the past three years. They'd endeared themselves to everyone by their cooperative and helpful attitudes.

During the military partnership, CME had matriculated four classes in three years. Everybody—students and faculty alike—were tired. Very tired.

In 1947 CME restored its 12-month curriculum. Class schedules and course sequences, which had been altered to accommodate the military, returned to normal. A very welcome peace and sense of normalcy replaced uncertainty among students and faculty.

Then Harold began addressing four priorities: sudden enrollment increase, admissions equity, dwindling faculty, and CME impact.

After the war, two to three times more qualified applicants—including women who'd been delayed—applied to CME than could be accepted. The sudden increase in applications had to be accommodated.

Procedures for selecting freshman medical students had to be reorganized, systematized, and based on fairness and equality. Charges of favoritism in the admission process had arisen.

During the war years, CME had lost more permanent faculty than it had gained. Standing barriers to the new-hire process were financial and philosophical concerns and the fact that CME employed only those who subscribed to Seventh-day Adventist beliefs and code of ethics.

Harold didn't even entertain the thought that he could accomplish these four goals alone. "We recognize that CME has been brought into existence under the Lord's guidance," he told his staff, "and has been divinely preserved in periods of great difficulty. I'm confident that the Lord will continue to protect and prosper this institution—if we retain our faith and trust in Him."

After the war, the demographics of CME's student population changed dramatically. More medical students were married, leaving Daniells Hall (the men's dormitory) far from full. Lindsay Hall (the women's dormitory) brimmed with nursing students. In order to accommodate incoming female applicants, CME assigned one floor of one wing of the men's dormitory to women medical students. The class preparing to graduate in 1950 was composed of almost 19 percent women, the largest percentage of female medical students since the first four classes starting in 1914 (which averaged almost 33 percent).

Protocols for the admission and advancement of medical students changed through the years. From the beginning CME's faculty council—the full-time basic science faculty—was responsible for selecting freshman medical students.

In time, the ability of CME to accept the most qualified students became suspect. The board of trustees voted to place the acceptance of freshman medical students in the hands of a board-appointed admissions committee instead of the faculty council. In addition to the evaluation of scholastic attainments, loyalty to Christian ideals became a subject of serious consideration.

Harold worked to create a more equitable plan for selecting freshman medical students. CME operated under unique ethical and religious ideals. Because of this, most applicants came from Adventist colleges throughout the country and it wasn't feasible for prospective students to make personal appearances before the admissions committee.

In order to develop a running account of year-by-year progress, Shryock preferred to become acquainted with premedical students in their undergraduate freshman year and visit them each year thereafter. In doing so, he became acquainted with the young men and women who hoped to apply at CME and was able to record the confidential appraisals made by trusted college faculty members, all the while promoting the good name of CME.

After arriving at a college campus, Shryock spent 20 minutes with each prospective medical student in a schedule organized by the registrar. He counseled them regarding their perspectives and choice of subjects, and he inquired about their scholastic progress, while typing his reflections and observations on his portable typewriter.

He challenged one student at PUC to improve his study habits and grades by telling him that, under present circumstances, he'd be a terrific candidate for the United States Army. That young man, Carleton Wallace, eventually became a 1956 graduate of CME, an orthopaedic surgeon, and Patti Shryock's husband.

After one interview, a student who apparently felt he'd failed to make a good impression rushed back into the room and announced, "Oh, Dr. Shryock, I forgot to tell you. I want to be a missionary!"

Shryock examined grades issued from the registrar's office. Recognizing the unreliability of his sole subjective impressions, he developed a plan whereby trusted individuals from each college who were personally acquainted with potential CME applicants could convey their appraisals to the CME admissions committee without being blamed if CME denied an applicant's admission. The list included science teachers, dormitory deans, dean of students, campus chaplain, or a representative of the Department of Religion.

Shryock developed a protocol that relayed CME's criteria for admissions, protected these trusted advisers from political intrusions, and kept communications confidential. At the close of each visit, he shared his typewritten interview impressions with the selected group of college teachers and recorded their reactions. In their presence he dictated a summary of how they responded. The transcriptions were made available to the CME admissions committee.

This protocol kept Shryock away from Loma Linda for several weeks during each school year. A loyal member of the faculty, Willard C. Fisher, M.D. (CME: 1939), shouldered Harold's routine duties whenever he was out of town.

Adventist college administrators treated Shryock as an honored guest. They often invited him to speak for chapel, and some students who weren't even planning to become physicians sought him out to discuss personal problems. Often they'd confide more freely in him than in local faculty members.

While taking Harold to the airport following a visit, one college president acknowledged the sensitivity of his interviews, adding, "Maybe some of the things you've learned, we ought to know." Maintaining his professional commitment to confidentiality, Harold found a creative way to change the subject.

During this time, Harold traveled 40,000 to 45,000 miles a year and traded his cars in at about 100,000 miles. To keep on schedule, Harold sometimes drove with a heavy foot. To maximize travel time, he dictated some of his reports and answered correspondence *while driving*. He also dictated book manuscripts under the same conditions.

He preferred traveling by car for a variety of reasons. He could carry his typewriter and heavy file folders in his trunk and didn't have to hire a taxi to transport him and his supplies to the mostly rural college campuses. While on the road, Harold ate on the run, sometimes buying provisions from country stores along the way; then, back on the road again, he'd enjoy his meal using a cracker as a spoon. When the cracker got soft, he'd eat it. No clean up!

Eventually Walter B. Clark became dean of students and Shryock gradually turned over the interviewing trips to him. The man who'd become dean as a matter of conscience had successfully led the campus through the difficult years of World War II. In good times and bad, during war and peace, Providence had been at work behind the scenes, guiding both Harold Shryock and his beloved CME.

Chapter 10

Family Matters

D uring the early years of their marriage, while Harold was becoming an effective force in the operation of the fledgling CME, Daisy proved to be an excellent wife and homemaker. Not only did she shape the lives of two growing children, but she also had a hand in shaping the life of the father of the house, sharpening Harold's perceptiveness in matters of family living and parenthood. Although sometimes strict, he also was patient, loving, and often entertaining.

Traditionally, mealtimes were happy occasions in the Shryock home, often punctuated with humor. Family prayers and a brief worship followed the evening meal. The entire clan carefully observed the Sabbath hours. Before sundown Friday night, the children polished their shoes and took their baths, while Daisy prepared the next day's meals.

Daisy often invited struggling students over for hearty helpings of split pea soup and tomato sandwiches. Over the years, she prepared food for many guests, including hobos who'd be given a big plate of nourishment and invited to sit on the front steps as they ate.

Some Friday evenings—when the town fire alarm interrupted meetings in Burden Hall, the main auditorium on campus used for both social and religious gatherings—proved more exciting than others. Usually the urgent call was in response to mischievous boys who set palm trees on fire in Loma Linda and Redlands. Whenever the whistle blew, it could be heard all over town. The first part of the alarm, a steam whistle, modulated from a high pitch to a low pitch, holding for a moment at both extremes. It sounded like an eerie air raid warning. Then a series of piercing blasts followed. The number of blasts corresponded with a section of town and told the volunteer firefighters where the action was. Fires were always a big deal. Shryock would hurriedly load his family in the car, and they'd head off trying to find the conflagration.

On Sabbath morning, the little family attended church services in Burden Hall. Harold and Daisy always tried to make Sabbath special for their children. They enjoyed picnics under their favorite trees in San Timoteo and Reche Canyons and, after eating, would stretch out and rest or go for bicycle rides. On occasion, they walked along the railroad tracks in Loma Linda or in San Timoteo Canyon, flattening pennies under the heavy steel wheels of passing trains.

The house on North San Bernardino Street provided the setting for many family memories. Harold enjoyed woodturning on a lathe set up in the basement, using his hobby as a form of diversional therapy that helped him unwind from the endless stresses of his job. He created candleholders and salt and pepper shakers from orangewood.

Across the street from their house stood a local orange grove (later removed for construction of Mortensen Hall, named after Harold's mentor and colleague Dr. Raymond Mortensen). When temperatures dropped, grove workers fired up oil-burning smudge pots to protect the fruit from freezing.

To fortify her home and family from the heavy, dark smoke, Daisy awakened the children and asked them to help her stuff newspapers under doors and cover furniture with sheets. Even with these precautions, many mornings found each member of the family sporting black nostrils. Their strange appearance wasn't too much of a shock to those in the neighborhood because everyone else in Loma Linda looked the same way.

When Eddy turned 15, the local orange grower hired him to light the fires on cold nights. The boy figured, *If you can't beat 'em, join 'em.*

Some memories weren't so fond, such as when Patti brought home mumps and shared them with her entire family. Harold suffered the most. Ethel Duncan, a registered nurse and the wife of Redlands physician Ray H. Duncan, M.D. (CME: 1942), stepped in to care for the uncomfortable, ailing bunch. During this time, several dignitaries arrived on campus to counsel with Harold about a pressing issue. The discussion simply couldn't wait. So they came to the Shryock home, made themselves comfortable on the front porch, and communicated through an open window. Inside, dressed in his bathrobe, carrying on the important work of the institution, sat swollen-necked, chipmunk-cheeked Harold.

Over the years, even students and parents were welcomed at the Shryock residence to talk about their problems. For particularly sensitive discussions, Harold would close the living room door, a signal for the children to stay away.

If one of his kids needed disciplining, Harold's Thursday evening trips to Los Angeles County General Hospital provided a perfect punishment time. Sometimes Harold took Patti. Sometimes he took Eddy. Whenever Daisy announced, "Your father wants to take you to Los Angeles on Thursday," both kids stopped whatever they were doing and wondered, *What did we do this time?*

On the trip into the city, Harold employed an indirect form of discipline. As they drove along, he'd relate a story illustrating someone else's family problem and its usually unpleasant outcome. The situation just happened to coincide with a current Shryock family issue, and the children could easily draw their own conclusions.

Sometimes everyone would ride into Los Angeles. Daisy and the kids would picnic in Hollenbeck Park and then wait at a curb by the hospital for Harold to emerge from his neurology meeting.

On one such outing, Harold's heavy foot caused an aromatic disaster. After picking up some embryos and an adult brain at the county hospital, he negotiated a corner too fast. The specimen jar overturned, spilling its contents. The powerful aroma of formaldehyde filled the vehicle. After securing the specimens, he continued the journey for 60 miles—with his family hanging out of the car windows, tears streaming from their eyes and wind blowing in their faces as each tried to escape the strong fumes—all the way back to Loma Linda.

Before Patti and Eddy became teenagers, Harold and Daisy took two more children into their care. Barry and Dolly Jean came from different broken homes, but they soon felt like part of the Shryock clan. Every morning proved challenging for Daisy to prepare a large breakfast, enjoy a brief worship, and keep everybody on time—especially in such a small residence.

Worships took place in the living room, where Harold sat in his favorite wicker rocking chair. Parts of the chair were coming unglued, and it squeaked in agony whenever its occupant rocked back and forth.

Tired of hearing their parents promise to get that piece of furniture repaired, the children decided to play a practical joke on the man who was constantly playing practical jokes on them. One evening the boys further loosened the already weak joints to the point where they knew the chair would collapse with little movement.

At the appointed time, Harold arrived for worship, Bible in hand, a serious expression on his face. The children held their breath as he sat down. Nothing happened. Harold started to read, while those sitting at his feet fought back giggles. The more they tried, the less they succeeded. At the first audible snicker, Harold became annoyed. "We can't have worship while you're giggling," he scolded. Satisfied that he'd laid down sufficient law, he started over. But the children continued creating nasal bursts of air as they fought to stay in control.

This time, Harold's exasperation level was more than exceeded. He sat forward to deliver his "keep still" command with added authority when, with a loud crunch and rapid series of snaps, the chair collapsed. The man with the Bible and the serious face landed on the floor in the middle of a debris field made up of what used to be a wicker rocker. The giggling broke into instant and uncontrolled laughter. Worship was definitely over.

Even though Harold enjoyed playing practical jokes as much as the next fellow, he was also a strict disciplinarian. When 14-year-old Patti got a D in citizenship, Harold marched her down to the academy to find out why. "We gave her that low grade for wearing pomade on her lips," he was told. Pomade, a slightly pink lip moisturizer, was popular with girls her age.

Harold turned to his daughter. "No more pomade," he stated firmly.

Soon thereafter, Patti succumbed to temptation. When she accidentally hurt her finger at school, she called her father to come pick her up. As she clamored into the car, trying to keep her throbbing appendage out of harm's way, Harold glanced at her pain-wrenched face and asked, "Ah, Patti, what do you have on your mouth?"

"Nothing," the girl responded, thinking that the offending color she'd applied earlier that day had certainly long vanished.

Harold reached into his pocket and pulled out his always clean, white handkerchief. "Wipe your lips," he ordered.

Harold Shryock
at 6 months
of age (1906).

Harold Shryock's birth
return from the
City of Seattle
Department of
Sanitation.

Harold Shryock
at age 5, with
his dog, Shep.

Background:
Loma Linda Sanitarium,
circa 1905.

Harold's parents, Alfred Q. Shryock,
M.D., and Stella Shryock.

Ellen G. White speaks at the dedication of the Loma Linda Sanitarium on April 15, 1906.

Left: Alfred Q. Shryock, M.D., his son, Harold, and wife, Stella, circa 1912.

Below: A major flood in 1916 undermined a home near Shryock's home, which was named Dew Drop Inn.

Background:
Class from the Nurses' Training School wearing the first cap.

The first graduating class from the Loma Linda Sanitarium Nurses' Training School. Seven members graduated in 1907 are looking at Richard Edward Abbott, infant son of George K. Abbott, M.D., the first dean of the CME School of Medicine.

Right: "Air-conditioned" Moore truck (seating capacity 21) transported student physicians to the San Bernardino County Hospital for clinical experience. Here, students and faculty are going to a medical/evangelist meeting. Dr. A. W. Truman, teacher of physiology and anatomy, and his wife, Daisy, sit in the middle of the third seat. Photo taken in 1913.

Alfred Q. Shryock, M.D., and his wife, Stella, teach a class in histology at CME.

A 21-year-old Harold Shryock meets a bear in Yosemite National Park.

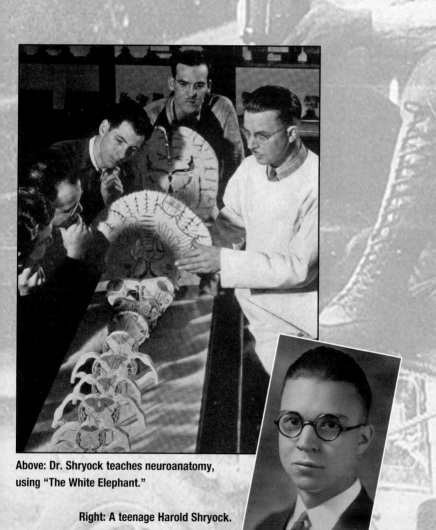

Above: Dr. Shryock teaches neuroanatomy, using "The White Elephant."

Right: A teenage Harold Shryock.

arold Shryock
joys a camping
p to Yosemite
Alfred Wical's
ely tuned
odel T Ford.

Background:
Lawrence Skinner, Alfred Wical,
and Harold Shryock upon their
return to Loma Linda from Pacific
Union College. Note the goggles
and the metal bucket hanging from
the windshield post.

Dubbed "Jericho" by medical students,
anatomy dissections for the College of
Medical Evangelists were conducted in
a corrugated sheet-metal building on the
south bank of the San Timoteo Creek,
about a quarter mile east of the Pepper
Drive—now Anderson Street—bridge.
It rested on a cement slab and was
well obscured by a surrounding
orange grove.

Background:
The new Loma Linda Sanitarium and Hospital were opened in April 1929.

Below: Daisy Bagwell graduated from the St. Helena Sanitarium School of Nursing in August 1927. She married Harold Shryock on April 30, 1929.

Bottom: E. Harold Shryock graduated in the Loma Linda Bowl from the College of Medical Evangelists on June 18, 1933.

Dr. Shryock and his wife, Daisy, pose with their daughter, Patti, and their son, Eddy.

The parlor of the Loma Linda Sanitarium and Hospital, opened in 1929.

Patti Shryock Wallace's favorite picture of her dad, Dr. Harold Shryock, working in his garden.

Alfred Q. Shryock, M.D., and his wife, Stella, parents of Dr. Harold Shryock.

Right: E. Harold Shryock, M.D., and his beloved Daisy.

Background:
Loma Linda University Medical Center,
circa 1970.

Harold and Daisy Shryock's family help
them celebrate their fiftieth wedding
anniversary on April 30, 1979.

Dr. and Mrs. Harold
Shryock were happily
married for 63 years.

The pink stain on the cloth exposed Patti's little secret. "You lied to me," he said, hurt filling his eyes. "You're not supposed to be wearing this stuff."

Harold didn't administer too many spankings, but the seriousness of this particular case motivated him to make an exception. The experience so humiliated Patti that she didn't speak to her dad for the rest of the day.

That evening, the Shryocks entertained dinner guests. After the meal, the unusually quiet Patti cleared the table and started washing dishes. Before long, Harold excused himself from the visitors in the living room and stepped into the kitchen. He picked up a dish towel and started drying the dishes. The two worked in silence for a long moment, the only sound filling the room was the splash of water and clank of china. Finally, the man said softly, "I just wanted to tell you I'm sorry that I had to do . . . what I did. But you lied to me."

Patti refused to respond.

Eventually, father and daughter made up. It was the last spanking Patti ever received.

Patti's acknowledgment of Harold's strictness proved politically expedient after she'd been voted vice president of her senior class of 1949. Unfortunately, the young class president had been impeached after admitting he'd participated in something the school considered harmful, an act that carried the "possibility of young people developing questionable relationships in a worldly environment." He'd gone bowling.

A fellow classmate was quickly voted in as replacement president. However, after suffering with a guilty conscience for three weeks, the second boy admitted, "I went bowling with him." This president was unceremoniously bounced out of office as well.

In an all-out effort to save the senior class from permanent disgrace, vice president Patti was asked if she went bowling, too. "No," Patti answered. Then she added the clincher. "Do you think, with a father like mine, I'd ever be caught dead in a bowling alley?" She was quickly sworn in as the third and final class president, a position she felt she'd earned by default.

⌒

Harold encouraged his children to be involved in sports and camping activities, played baseball with them, and took them horseback riding. One experience proved a test of the family's faith.

On a clear, bright Sunday, the Shryocks went horseback riding in a canyon near Grand Terrace. The physician who owned the horses went along for the ride. Toby, the Shryocks' springer spaniel, also started out as the riders took off. Toby loved going places; however, she was lazy.

As the ride progressed, the temperature rose. Toby, who suffered from a chronic lack of exercise, would periodically lie down and rest. Toward noon somebody in the group noticed that the little dog was missing. As soon as the riders got back to the stables, the owner took one of the horses and quickly retraced their steps, even checking the concrete-lined Gage Canal that traversed the area.

No Toby.

With heavy hearts, the family went home and Daisy contacted a local radio station, which announced Toby's disappearance.

After eating lunch, Patti and Eddy decided that more help was needed in their efforts to locate the missing dog. So the two knelt and prayed, sharing their deep concern with God and expressing faith that their prayers would be answered. Then they came up with a plan.

"Daddy, you hike up the east end of the little canyon, go over the top, retracing the morning ride in reverse. Then meet us back at the stable."

Harold grabbed a long leash and quart jar filled with water, ready to offer the certainly-by-now-very-thirsty animal some refreshment. But, when he reached the end of the canyon, there was still no sign of the missing dog.

Believing that his children's faith was at stake, Harold knelt alone on the trail and poured out his heart to God, asking Him to reward the simple trust of his children. When he opened his eyes, there stood Toby, facing him on the trail.

The animal eagerly drank the water, and then the two hurried back to the stables. The children didn't act surprised when Toby appeared at the end of their father's leash. After all, hadn't they asked the God of the universe for help?

⌒

At first, the Shryocks rented horses for riding. Then they bought one.

When they took in Barry and Dolly Jean, they bought a second horse and pastured India and Ginger along the southwest bank of the San Timoteo Creek, behind the Loma Linda Elementary School. Daily chores for the four children included caring for the horses, feeding them oats, and making sure they had plenty of water to drink.

In 1947, while Harold was out of town, the community fire alarm sounded in the middle of the night. Because the coded alarm placed the fire in the vicinity of the school, Daisy awakened the children. "I think we'd better go down and see how the horses are," she announced.

When the group arrived, dressed in their nightclothes with grain and bridles in hand, they found that the horses were just fine. But the school wasn't faring as well. It was totally engulfed in flames. Traumatized, the children stood watching part of their school burn to the ground, knowing that their books, lockers, and personal belongings were in it. All they could do was cry.

Horse ownership led to frog ownership. Eddy enjoyed digging in the backyard and, one cool February day, scooped out a large hole and filled it with water. Into this newly created pond he dumped a bucketful of pollywogs, a treasure he'd collected from puddles in the horse pasture. "Keep this hole filled with water while I'm at school," he instructed his mother.

It wasn't long before frogs were all over the yard, some making their escape out on the street. Mrs. Butterfield, the Shryocks' neighbor, didn't exactly share Eddy's excitement at successfully re-creating one of the plagues of Egypt.

~

When Daisy accompanied Harold on one of his many trips, a family friend would sometimes supervise Patti and Eddy. Volga Ward, wife of R. Leslie Ward, M.D. (CME: 1930), was on active duty when Eddy invited one of his friends to go target practicing on a hill overlooking the nearby Montecito Memorial Park. The boys decided to shoot some rounds into a small reservoir to check their weapons' accuracy. The noise they created caused some excitement in the nearby cemetery. From their vantage point they noticed two stern-faced men hop into their cars and start patrolling the nearby roads.

"I think we're in trouble," Eddy breathed to his companion.

The two friends stashed their guns in an old irrigation ditch, waited until dark, then sneaked down the hill, crossed Barton Road, and crawled on their hands and knees in a ditch until they were opposite Eddy's parked car. Carefully, the boy pulled the keys from his pocket, then whispered, "OK, run!"

Eddy's trembling fingers prevented him from inserting the key. As he frantically fumbled with the lock, a man emerged from a nearby walnut grove and reached into his pocket. "He's got a gun," Eddy gasped. When the stranger's hand emerged holding a pen and paper, Eddy almost fainted with relief. "What are your names?" the man called, rapidly closing the distance between him and the boys.

At that moment, the car door opened and the two teenagers jumped into the vehicle. Before the stranger could react, they raced away.

In his rearview mirror, Eddy saw a new Pontiac skid to a stop beside the mystery man, pick him up, and start following them as they sped down the road. The boys headed up Reche Canyon with headlights and taillights off and spotlight on. Then they turned off the highway and bumped and skidded east through the weeds, toward an area known as the clay pits. Because Eddy had ridden horses through those hills, he knew the trails and roads well. He also knew how to get around a gate that finally stopped the Pontiac in its tracks.

While the good dean and his wife served God's institution miles away from Loma Linda, their son was on the lam. Eddy and his buddy drove through the hills on a power line road—feeling as if they were fugitives— to the present location of Hulda Crooks Park, at the end of Mountain View Avenue. Emerging from an orange grove, they parked their dirt-and-dust-stained car in Alfred's garage and then tried to walk home as if nothing had happened.

When they came through the front door of Eddy's house, faithful Mrs. Ward, totally unaware of the day's drama, presented them with a delicious supper.

While the boys sat eating, the doorbell rang. Eddy peaked through the curtains and his breath stopped in his chest. At the curb sat a police car, a U.S. marshal's car, and the new Pontiac. "Yes, a young man from this house went hunting this afternoon," he heard Mrs. Ward tell the visitor, "Why do you ask?"

The stranger asked a few more questions and then took up positions with the others in their cars. Apparently, none of the pursuers realized that their quarry had beaten them home and were sitting in another room of the house eating supper.

Eddy and his buddy waited until after the cars left and then asked the still oblivious Mrs. Ward to take them to the Medical Cadet Corps meeting that night at the academy. Afterward, as they made their way home, they came to the conclusion that all was right with the world.

They were wrong.

The next morning, during study hall at Loma Linda Union Academy, the librarian tapped Eddy and his friend on their shoulders. "You're wanted in the principal's office," she whispered.

Down the hall, they were greeted by a U.S. marshal, who immediately took them to the Redlands Police Department for fingerprinting. Then they found themselves standing before Judge Van Unger in Loma Linda. "Well, my young friends," the man said, leaning forward and smiling down at them from behind his tall desk, "why don't you tell me what you've been up to."

The two captured fugitives did their best to explain the events of the previous day. After they finished, the judge thought for a minute and then said, "Sorry, boys. Discharging firearms in that area is illegal. You were also trespassing, causing a public disturbance, and took flight when authorities tried to stop you. I'm going to have to take your guns away from you for two weeks. After that time, you can come back and get them."

Both young men agreed that their sentence was a whole lot better than being thrown in jail.

Over the years, the Shryock children never saw anything but love in Harold's response to their frequent and sometimes very creative misbehavior. His reaction to one event made such a positive impression that Eddy never forgot it.

The teenager got a job working in the sanitarium kitchen, washing dishes, pots, pans, and trays for 80 cents an hour. One evening, a buddy asked, "If I help you, would you be interested in coming down to my place to have some fun?"

"Sure," Eddy responded.

After work, as he hung up his dishrag, Eddy said, "So, what's up for tonight?

His companion leaned forward. "Let's head down to the Tri-City Drive-in Theater and see what's playing."

In Adventist circles, going to movies was a grievous misuse of time, about the worst thing anybody could even think of doing.

Under cover of night, the two climbed over the drive-in wall and made themselves comfortable by some unoccupied speakers. After a while, because it was getting late, they decided they'd better head back to their homes.

Just as they strolled onto the friend's driveway, a pair of headlights snapped on, illuminating the two teenagers like searchlights revealing a prison break. Eddy heard the car door open, and soon a figure stood silhouetted by the brilliant beams. "Where have you fellows been?" a familiar voice asked. It was Harold.

Eddy's friend quickly vanished, leaving father and son facing each other.

Eddy hung his head. "We went to the movies, Dad," he said. "The drive-in. It . . . it was my friend's idea."

The two stood in silence. Then Eddy heard his father sigh. "Son," the man said, "I'll quit my job and move away from this town if it will help you choose better friends."

The words cut like a knife. Eddy knew his father loved CME and had dedicated his life to its success. Now this amazing man was offering to move, leave it all behind, for the sake of his son. His father's gentle rebuke that night would stay with him for the rest of his life.

☞

Harold constantly looked for ways to relate positively to his son. Both loved cars, so their conversations often centered on driving skills and automobiles. When Eddy enrolled in a class in auto mechanics at the academy, he discovered an article in *Popular Mechanics* focusing on a way to increase power in internal combustion engines. *Hmmm,* the boy thought, *Dad's brand-new 1949 Mercury sure doesn't have much oomph.*

According to the article, to increase the engine's output, one merely needed to "shave" the cylinder heads. That little modification would increase the cylinder's compression and result in more get-up-and-go!

Eddy presented his bright idea to his dad. "I'm all in favor of getting more pep out of this vehicle," the man responded. "And," he added, "we can do the project together. Father and son."

The would-be mechanics milled the heads 40 thousandths of an inch, and then reassembled the engine. Sure enough, the car ran much better—for a while. Then, because the heads were now closer to the valves, the valves burned, leaving the car with less compression and a lot less power than it had originally. But at least this time, the two Shryocks had learned a valuable lesson *together*. Eddy's deep fascination with the automobile remained a bright spot. He continued to enjoy this particular passion throughout his lifetime and, as an adult, it provided mobility that was vital to his career. It also became an interest he could share with his own children in coming years.

During a rare time when Harold was caught up with his work, Daisy suggested that he and Eddy go on a father-son vacation and "just talk." "He's a restless teenager and needs special attention," she told her husband. "Maybe you can instill in our son some much-needed wisdom."

When Harold asked Eddy if he wanted to go on a trip with him, a *real* trip without work and business appointments, the boy jumped at the idea. "Sure," he responded with a broad grin. "Where will we go?"

The two decided to take Grandpa Shryock's old 1939 Dodge sedan down into Mexico. They'd carry their own water, camp out, and prepare meals. Harold, ever the educator, gave Eddy a lesson in contacting country officials to have the trip authorized by the Mexican consulate in San Bernardino.

For some time, Eddy wanted to sport a short haircut like the rest of the guys, but Mother and Grandmother always objected. So he hit upon a plan. He asked his dad to take along the family hair clippers, the device Harold had been using for years to give curly-haired Eddy his every-other-week trim.

"But," Harold countered, "there'll be no electricity where we're going."

"No problem," his son said with a grin. "I've seen you run your dictation equipment off the car battery using an inverter. I figure you can hook up the ol' electric hair clippers the same way, right?"

Harold frowned. "You want me to take you to Mexico and give you a haircut?"

"Sure, why not?"

Once across the California-Mexico border, father and son experienced culture shock: buying gasoline in liters instead of gallons, paying in pesos instead of dollars, and driving kilometers instead of miles.

That evening, after exploring the countryside, the two tired travelers found a beautiful campsite at the end of a dirt road near a steep, seaside bluff. In the distance they could hear the waves crashing on stones below, a rhythmic sound that lulled them to sleep under a brilliant canopy of stars.

The next morning, after enjoying a hearty breakfast, they hiked down to the bottom of the 100-foot bluff and explored the rocks and pools left by the retreating tide. They were alone together. For hours their voices rang out in the pristine environment. "Hey, look at this," one would say. "I've never seen this kind of creature," the other would offer. At their feet waited dozens of interesting life forms—starfish, jelly-fish, assorted crustaceans. . . .

As the hot sun began to heat their exposed necks and arms, Harold stretched tired muscles and called over to his son, "Well, what do you want to do now?"

"How 'bout that haircut," his son replied.

Harold shook his head. "We're in beautiful, enchanting, mysterious Mexico surrounded by exotic creatures and a fascinating culture, and you want me to give you a haircut?"

"Oh, not just any haircut," the boy said, walking up to his father. "Give me one of those buzzies like my friends wear. Just cut it all off! It'll be fun. OK, Dad?"

Harold grinned and nodded his head. "Well, OK, if that's what you want. And you can give me one, too."

"A buzzie?"

"No, no!" the older man laughed. "Just a regular one, like my friends wear."

So it was, under a steaming Mexican sun, clippers hooked up to the old car's battery, that Eddy got his long-wished-for flattop. Harold had a little taken off over the ears.

Days later, when showing off his new hairdo to admiring schoolmates, they asked where he'd gone to get such a great cut. "Oh, my dad did it on a camping trip the two of us took to Mexico."

"Your dad!" the boys gasped.

Eddy smiled. "Sure. You don't know him like I do."

Hearing of this exchange from an adult friend, Harold gratefully acknowledged that the purpose of the trip had been well fulfilled.

As descendants of the socially influential Harold and Alfred Shryock, Patti and Eddy found that bearing the Shryock name brought them both positive and negative experiences. Patti and Eddy were attending PUC during the time that Harold interviewed premed students on campus. Some shined up to Patti, hoping to influence her dad through her. Others feared her, probably thinking she might speak a word against them. She and Eddy made a pact that they'd never discuss with their father anyone they knew who'd applied for medical school.

All except Carleton Wallace.

Patti's relationship with another young man she'd agreed to marry was in trouble. She knew in her heart that their romantic involvement was, in fact, over.

After returning late from a spring break, she stood in the bookstore trying to gather the required materials for her secretarial, business, and home economics classes when she heard someone call her name. "How are things going?" a handsome young man asked as he came up beside her.

"Not really great," Patti answered, recognizing the smiling face of her ex-fiancé's roommate.

"Well," said Carleton, a young man eager to take up any slack in Patti's social life, "if I can be of any help, let me know."

"Sure, thanks." Patti had no interest in pursuing romantic leads. The pain of her last relationship was still too fresh.

But Carleton operated under no such handicap and, when the time seemed right, asked Patti for a date. To the happy astonishment of both, she accepted.

Their first outing ended in disaster. On a warm March evening in 1951, Patti and Carleton joined five other couples, sneaked off campus, and, under a full moon, went swimming in the large, community pool in the center of the resort town of Calistoga.

When college authorities learned of the unauthorized outing, they were not impressed and suspended everyone involved. The group also found themselves "social bound" for three weeks for mixed swimming. Patti wrote her parents and explained what had happened. Harold and Daisy couldn't believe their eyes. Patti? Suspended? *Patti?*

During her senior year, she became the social vice president of the student association. The year before, she'd been vice president of her junior class and president of the Women of Alpha Gamma, the dormitory women's club. "She sure doesn't get her social skills from me," Harold told friends. "Patti's social aptitude certainly comes from the genes she inherited from her mother"—the little unnamed orphan baby girl who smiled and held up her arms to Jenny Bagwell.

In the autumn of 1951, the Shryocks received a letter from Patti that included these words. "I have a new boyfriend. He's good looking, genteel, and speaks with a Southern accent."

The Shryocks responded with a letter of their own. "Invite him to come to Loma Linda for a visit."

She did. They liked him.

However, at one point in Patti and Carleton's developing relationship, Daisy offered some one-on-one, straightforward advice to the good looking and genteel Mr. Wallace. "If you're serious about our daughter," she told him in private, "that's fine. But if you're not, move on!"

Carleton got the message loud and clear and decided that it might be a very good idea to get his hands on an engagement watch as quickly as possible.

Patricia Shryock and Carleton Wallace were married on August 16, 1953. Patti had just graduated from PUC, and Carleton had completed his first year as president of his freshman medical class at CME and was about to begin his sophomore year. Dean Walter Clark officiated.

In anticipation of the happy event, Patti and Carleton rented an apartment and spent their spare time sprucing it up. Two or three days before the wedding, Harold noticed a bunch of keys that had been left on top of the family radio. Recognizing them as belonging to his beautiful daughter, he slipped them into his pocket and made a quick visit to Dio's Key Shop in San Bernardino, where he had a copy made of the key that fit the new apartment's front door. Then he returned the set before they were missed.

After the newlyweds left for their honeymoon trip, Harold and Eddy headed for Carleton and Patti's new apartment. Sure enough, the new key worked. Then they stood looking at each other, trying to decide on the perfect welcome home gift for the newlyweds.

This thought was weighing heavily on their minds while they shopped at the local Thrifty Drugstore. Suddenly, they came across the answer.

With growing excitement, the two practical jokers bought two cartons of photographic flashbulbs. These bulbs looked like any ordinary incandescent bulb, except they had a wad of magnesium foil inside instead of a filament. They also screwed into any ordinary light socket.

Acting like children at play, Harold and Eddy replaced all the incandescent light bulbs in the apartment with flashbulbs. They even unfastened the ceiling fixture and installed a flashbulb there, too. Then, to make sure that the couple would feel totally welcomed, they short-sheeted their bed.

When Patti and Carleton got back with glowing reports of their honeymoon, Harold and Daisy listened impatiently, waiting for the couple to head for their apartment. Eddy wasn't home that evening, and Daisy knew of the welcome awaiting her daughter and her new husband.

As soon as Carleton and Patti left the house, the Shryocks jumped into their car and headed for a good vantage point, where they could watch the events about to unfold.

The tired but happy newlyweds parked their car at the curb and hauled their suitcases up the walk to the entrance to their apartment. Carleton unlocked the door and reached inside to turn on the living room light. Instantly, a flash lit up the whole neighborhood. Then, total darkness. The two hurried inside, closing the door behind them. Suddenly, a second brilliant flash streamed through all the windows. And then another . . . and another.

Nearby, the two observers were gasping for breath as uncontrollable laughter rocked their car.

⌒

Harold's sense of humor found many outlets. On one occasion, good ol' Dad appeared at his daughter's front door with a large, neatly wrapped package with Patti's name on it. "Somebody here having a birthday?" he called.

As he walked into the room, he suddenly tripped, fumbled the box like a football player trying to contain a wayward pass, and watched in horror as it crashed to the floor with all of the appropriate tinkling sound effects of a very expensive accident.

"Oh dear, oh dear," Harold gasped. "I feel terrible!" Turning to his speechless daughter he added, "I'm so sorry, Patti. I'm sure whatever was in there was very nice."

When she could move, Patti rushed to examine the remains of her treasure. She found the box filled with discarded pottery, some old dishes, and a huge rock. Patti's actual present, a new set of dishes, was safe and sound in the next room, right where Harold had put them earlier.

In spite of Harold's busy schedule, he and Daisy placed great significance on their family. Whether traveling across country, hot-rodding an engine with Eddy, fumbling Patti's "present," teaching his children responsibility, or pleading with God to answer their prayers for a lost dog, Harold's every action echoed, "You're important to me—I love you."

Harold also felt continuously uplifted by his stimulating relationship with Daisy, the wife of his youth. This vivacious, Spirit-filled woman influenced his career, avocations, and parental activities more than any other person.

In the hand of Providence, he'd found guidance and purpose. He'd also discovered an endless source of blessings.

Chapter 11

Transitions, Challenges, and Rewards

arold Shryock served as dean of the Loma Linda division from 1945 to 1950, associate dean from 1950 to 1951, and dean from 1951 to 1954. As teacher and dean, he often overcame challenges and confronted situations that permanently impacted the lives of his students.

In 1942 Shryock asked two of his students how each of them studied. The conversation was reported by Ronald C. Gregory, M.D., at a class reunion during the 2004 Annual Postgraduate Convention. "Oh, we hit the books right after supper," they reported. "We don't go out for a half-hour volleyball game. We study straight to at least 11:00 before turning in. If we haven't covered the assignment by bedtime, we set the alarm for 4:00 and study, sometimes straight through breakfast. We don't close the books till we enter the first morning class."

"I see," Shryock responded. "No wonder you two are failing. Remember, the brain can't remain fully alert for more than one hour at a time," he advised. "Stop at the end of 50 minutes and take a breather. Run around the block for 10 minutes, then sit down for another session of study. Go listen to the radio for news for 10 minutes. Then quit the study period and go to bed by 10:00. If you haven't covered the assignment, it is OK to get up at 4:00, but don't ever skip breakfast. When you go to your first class, spend the last 15 minutes talking about the weather or any subject other than your review of the last night's study period."

Because of the war effort, both finished their accelerated medical course in record time—37 months—from September 4, 1941, to October 1944. Most of their vacation time between the nine months of study had been deleted.

Harold gave more advice to the first class admitted into the School of Dentistry. During his orientation lecture in 1953, he described methods of study that former students had found successful. He gave valuable advice about times of day that are most conducive to memorization and comprehension. The student should get up at sunrise and prepare the body and mind by morning devotions, followed by a wholesome breakfast. Immediately afterward, first thing in the morning, study.

☞

Some of Harold's work-created stress related to the subject of fairness and his basic sense of right and wrong. In one particular situation, it concerned an applicant who was not accepted into the School of Medicine.

A subcommittee of the school board called Harold in to face a possible reprimand. The applicant in question—a foreign premedical student from the Middle East—had been accepted into PUC. The young man had no particular knowledge of the Seventh-day Adventist Church or the ideals or mission heralded by CME. Shryock began counseling him when he was a freshman at PUC, continuing to do so for four years.

Right from the start, the young man's scholastic achievements proved strikingly unacceptable. As a courtesy, and in order to deal fairly and honestly with the student, Shryock confronted him during his second interview with a rather unsettling fact of life. "CME gives preference to members of the Adventist Church in a manner similar to the preference a state medical school gives to its own citizens," he told him. "In addition to your unacceptable grades, you have a disadvantage because you don't hold membership in the church that supports CME." Harold hoped that, by sharing this information early in his premedical education, the young man would have ample time to apply at a medical school where his church membership, or lack thereof, wouldn't be an issue.

Harold stared intently at the student. "There have been cases," he said, "in which students have been tempted to join the Adventist church, just so they'd be accepted into CME. My advice to you is: Let your conscience be your guide."

Harold was surprised to find the young man still hopeful, during his junior year at PUC, of being admitted to CME. Instead of acknowledging his handicap and moving on, the student joined the church and engineered political moves with visiting church leaders designed to bypass Harold's counsel and orchestrate his own entrance into the Loma Linda medical school, despite unacceptable grades. He even told his professors that he wanted to become a medical missionary to his non-Christian country.

Over the years, CME had in fact admitted outstanding, scholastically qualified non-Adventists. But the admissions committee rejected the young man's application, based on his unacceptable grades and low score on his Medical College Admissions Test (MCAT). It was a routine decision based on an objective evaluation of the facts.

During Shryock's next visit to PUC, the young man expressed his great disappointment. "You shouldn't be surprised," Harold countered. "I pointed out to you during our interview last autumn that your grades were so low that there was no reasonable prospect of your being accepted."

Shortly thereafter, Shryock received a letter from William H. Branson, president of the General Conference of Seventh-day Adventists, and cosigned by a vice president, requesting that the admissions committee give favorable reconsideration to this particular student's application. Church leaders felt he offered potential evangelistic possibilities for medical missionary work in his home country—a worthy expectation considering the strong evangelistic mission of the denomination. Branson also happened to be a member of the CME board of trustees.

While being sympathetic to the church leader's concerns, Harold felt obligated to be fair to all qualified applicants. He responded with a detailed and lengthy letter, reporting the young man's unacceptable grade point average and MCAT score. "The student in question would be unable to earn even passing grades in medical school," he concluded, quoting statistics to validate the committee's decision.

Before long, Harold received an understanding reply from the vice president who'd cosigned the original request. The man agreed with his conclusion, and Harold considered the matter closed.

But before the next board meeting convened, Macpherson asked Shryock to attend a special committee. "Bring that Middle Eastern student's folder," he added.

During the closed-door session, Branson asked if the admissions committee had addressed his request for favorable reconsideration. "No,"

Harold answered, "we haven't had any admissions committees recently, and our work is done for this year."

Then he presented the letter he'd received in answer to his response—the letter that had led him to conclude that the matter was closed. "I didn't know that letter [the vice president's response] had ever been written," replied Branson. The mood of the meeting suddenly changed.

Walter Beach, secretary of the General Conference and also a member of the board, asked to see Harold's detailed response. In it, he had portrayed the unfairness of depriving a qualified applicant in order to accommodate a person with political pull. "This is a good letter," stated Beach.

By the end of the session, Harold stood vindicated in sparing the admissions committee the influences of outside political forces—no matter how worthy the cause.

⊂

Shryock and his CME family experienced light moments as well. One day Harold invited Francis D. Nichol, editor of the denomination's *Life and Health* magazine, to deliver an impromptu speech at chapel. Nichol often came to Loma Linda to visit his aged parents, who resided on the hill in the Sanitarium Annex. Nichol had lived on campus when his dad served as engineer in charge of the boiler housed in the original sanitarium.

He had another reason for coming to Southern California. Over the years, he'd developed a great fondness for Daisy's boysenberry pie.

During one stopover, Nichol held reservations on the Santa Fe Superchief, the high-speed train that passed through San Bernardino before continuing on to Washington, D.C. It made its stop at exactly the same time the chapel program began in Burden Hall. Realizing that the train would have a slow ascent up the Cajon Pass as it headed for the high desert, Shryock came up with a plan. "If you speak to the students, I'll make sure you get on that train in Barstow."

Shryock loved fast cars, earning the nickname *Jehu*. Jehu, a biblical king of Israel, enjoyed a reputation for driving his chariot "furiously" (2 Kings 9:20). To keep his promise, Harold would have to race the *Superchief* up the mountain to Barstow and do it in decidedly biblical fashion.

Nichol agreed to speak because he relished the idea of addressing future physicians. When introducing the editor as a true friend of medical students, Harold added, "If you need proof that our guest speaker has a deep interest in you, consider this fact: Right at this moment, the train on which he has reservations to go to Washington, D.C., is leaving the station in San Bernardino." Outside in the parking lot, Shryock's maroon 1946 Ford, with Nichol's suitcase already tucked in the trunk, sat waiting.

When Francis arrived at the podium, he called out, "I am reminded of a remark made by gladiators as they faced the spectators before the fight began: 'We, who are about to die, salute you.' " A roar of laughter erupted from the gathered medical students.

Nichol spoke for 30 minutes. Then he and Harold headed for the Cajon Pass, chasing the steel tracks that wound up the mountain. Shryock kept his word and then some. They stood in Barstow for 15 minutes, waiting for the train to arrive.

When he returned to campus, everyone he met asked the same question. "Dr. Shryock, did you make it?"

⌒

In time, Harold, the softhearted peacemaker, found it increasingly difficult to don his administrative hardhat and do battle each day with the issues facing the facility. "I'm not the type of personality who can do dean's work without considerable expenditure of nervous energy," he told his staff. "I'm beginning to run low on nervous energy."

On June 30, 1954, after 10 years of service, Harold notified the board chair that he needed to be replaced, and he resigned as dean.

In a handwritten letter dated September 5, President Macpherson responded, "I have appreciated more than I can state or put down adequately in writing your performance as dean of the School of Medicine," he said. "Your careful and accurate analysis and handling of many difficult as well as routine matters have been very comforting to me. Your sound judgment has been so consistent as to have become a well-recognized quality. . . . Thank you for your many years of service to CME."

In *Around the Circuit,* a newsletter to CME personnel, Macpherson further stated that Shryock had been CME's ambassador of goodwill and had taken a deep personal interest in contributing to better techniques for selecting outstanding students each year from SDA colleges across the nation.

In a letter dated October 11, 1954, Dr. Godfrey T. Anderson, president of La Sierra College, added his appreciation for the great work that Harold had done. "I think that I can speak for the administrators of our liberal arts colleges when I say that we have found you, in all of our dealings, to be all that we could ask of a person in this position. During the days when you were flooded with applications, both our students and our faculty felt that you . . . handled matters with dispatch [and] that you were completely objective and fair in all your dealings with these young people."

Humbly, Harold acknowledged that he would definitely miss the many intimate contacts he'd experienced with educators throughout the denomination, interactions he found both enjoyable and stimulating. However, his first love was education.

What would Harold do? He had several job opportunities, but preferred to teach anatomy. As dean he had supervised Dr. Otto Kampmeier, the chair of the Department of Anatomy. If he returned to the department, Kampmeier would supervise him. Would that present a problem? In consultation, President Macpherson suggested that Harold visit Kampmeier, who was on a three-month summer vacation at his home in Wisconsin, to find out. Following pleasantries and a brief discussion, Kampmeier welcomed Harold back into the Department of Anatomy.

"Now that I'm back in the classroom and laboratory serving as associate professor of anatomy," he wrote to friends, "I'm coming to realize, again, the very tangible satisfactions that come from personal contacts with students."

Shryock also accepted teaching assignments in various other subjects. On July 1, 1957, he became professor of anatomy and chair of the Department of Anatomy, a position he held for the next 12 years. Because dental students also studied anatomy, Harold became a member of the faculty of the School of Dentistry. As such, from 1961 to 1968 he participated in eight annual meetings of the National Board of Dental Examiners in Chicago, and played his part well by developing new questions each year on the subject of histology and embryology.

$$\infty$$

Believing that it was God who had placed him in a position of enormous responsibility—whether upholding the unique rules of a conservative institution, protecting its admissions committee from political influences, or strengthening its staff and resources—Harold Shryock conscientiously guided his beloved alma mater while trusting the hand of Providence.

Chapter 12

Writing–A Second Calling

lthough Harold Shryock wore many professional hats during his lifetime, he's best known internationally as an author. During his career, he became the most prolific Adventist physician-writer for lay readers in the denomination since John Harvey Kellogg, M.D., penning a vast array of books, magazine articles, advice columns, and reports for *The [Alumni] Journal*.

Harold's interest in writing began in the ninth grade. His teacher, Miss Mabel Andre, an English major fresh out of college, taught ninth-grade composition and tenth-grade rhetoric. Some of her students became interested in writing as a direct result of her thoughtful instruction.

Harold and his classmates tried to tease Miss Andre by writing on themes such as "Are Ladies Safe Drivers?" They heard via the grapevine that Miss Andre and her sister, a medical student, as well as their widowed father fully enjoyed reading their insightful papers.

PUC's courses in public speaking had little to do with writing, but did involve translating thoughts into words. These classes, in a way, helped develop Harold's future journalistic skills. He found himself associating with English majors and acquiring some of their interest in putting pen to paper. In medical school Harold gave top priority to the study of science and put aside the pursuit of writing, except for case histories. Later, as a teacher, he produced syllabus books on various topics for his classes. This effort challenged him to create stimulating learning experiences for his students.

Then, one day, a unique combination of interests came together and launched Harold's writing career. While teaching freshman medical students, he discovered he was in fact holding down two jobs: lecturer as well as counselor, encouraging students in their adjustments to medical school and transitions to professional life. In this capacity, he was exposed to the wide range of scholastic pressures, financial difficulties, and marital conflicts that plague young people. His one-on-one conversations with them in the quiet of his office provided real-world insights into some of the difficulties they endured. Harold's ongoing attempts to help his students untangle their personal problems drove him to a deeper study of human relations, mental health, personality problems, and human psychology.

Publication of a manuscript by the widely read *Youth's Instructor* (January 1, 1935) gave Harold some encouragement that his articles could help young people and were greatly needed. Also, during the '40s and '50s, his personal relationship with Francis D. Nichol, editor of *Life and Health* magazine, broadened into a professional one as well.

One day he asked his friend, "Francis, do you think I could supplement my income by writing? My children will soon be off to academy and college, where tuition isn't exactly cheap. I could certainly use some extra pennies in my bank account."

Nichol responded with enthusiasm. "Tell you what," he said, "why don't you prepare a series of articles for *Life and Health* magazine? That ought to get the ball rolling."

So it was that, beginning in July 1944, Nichol published a series of 14 Harold Shryock articles dealing mainly with the psychological barriers to success such as anxiety, fear, worry, troublesome moods, and lack of self-confidence.

Even while that series was being released in the magazine, Harold asked his friend about the possibility of writing another. Nichol hesitated only a moment. "We need some articles about the family."

Harold prepared an eight-part series highlighting home relations and how to enjoy a successful marriage. Based on his observations of freshman medical students and the courses he'd taken in psychology, the articles focused on mutual regard, patience, forbearance, and a commitment to get along.

Eventually, with continuing encouragement from friend Francis, Harold expanded those articles into a full-blown, 22-chapter book entitled *Happiness for Husbands and Wives*.

First published in 1949, and eventually printed in several languages over a period of 20 years, the volume emphasized marriage as a sacred privilege that enabled spouses to blend their lives in loyalty to each other and to their Creator.

Harold focused on how to avoid illness and promote health and well-being. In his magazine articles, such as "Can Sickness Originate in the Mind?" "Can Emotional Problems Injure the Organs?" "Are You Afraid of Fear?" and "Manifestations of Functional Disease," he stressed that a person's positive thoughts and attitudes promote health—and that negative emotions can create physical disease.

Once in print, Harold boldly decided that his articles could have an even broader influence if incorporated into a book. He'd add and update material from his syllabus for the psychobiology course for freshman medical students, including his materials on mental processes such as perception, memory, imagination, and decision-making.

In 1948, when the editors at Pacific Press Publishing Association encouraged him to compile his wealth of material into a book, he organized a manuscript with 31 chapters. Pacific Press accepted the project on February 14, 1950, and published it under the title *Happiness and Health*.

Encouraged, Shryock explored suitable book ideas with the other Adventist publishers. Leadership at Review and Herald Publishing Association, in Takoma Park, Maryland, suggested that books on adolescent adjustment to adulthood—targeting ages 12 to 18—would do well. Harold suggested two separate books for young people that would address sexual issues frankly and factually. The editors liked Shryock's suggestions and invited him to produce the manuscripts. *On Becoming a Man* and *On Becoming a Woman,* published by the Review and Herald in the early 1950s, became best sellers.

By this time, Harold was interviewing prospective medical students at the Adventist colleges. With the help of a friend who was a skilled electrician, he had equipped his car with an inverter so that his vehicle battery could power a dictating machine while he drove. Although it took a bit of concentration, he could dictate a chapter a day. His transcriber sometimes reported hearing squealing brakes in the background.

In September 1950, J. D. Snider, manager of the Book Department of the Review and Herald, asked Harold to create a manuscript for their new *Highways* series—a set of books that presented various phases of successful Christian living. Harold's book *Highways to Health* would be teamed with

C. L. Paddock's book *Highways to Happiness,* because colporteurs were finding it easier to sell sets of books rather than single volumes. Snider urged Shryock to come up with the new manuscript as quickly as possible.

Because of Harold's involvement with other unfinished manuscripts and his workload as dean at CME, he decided to collaborate with a colleague, Dr. Mervyn Hardinge. The two physicians began the project by developing a table of contents of 46 chapters. They agreed to write the manuscript in simple language for lay readers, each chapter beginning with a short series of questions to be answered in subsequent pages. Their book would have a spiritual flavor without focusing on specific doctrines; almost 10 percent of the 340 pages would contain illustrations.

Then in August 1952, Hardinge accepted an unusual opportunity for postgraduate training. He gave Harold permission to use the material he'd already prepared. Thanks to his colleague's cooperation and the enterprising involvement of Patti, who served as secretary for the project, Shryock submitted the completed manuscript to the Review and Herald on September 28, 1952.

During the next four years, the best-selling *Highways to Health* was translated into Norwegian, French, Spanish, and Portuguese.

In 1955 Shryock's previous book, *Happiness and Health,* was translated into Finnish and published with an introduction by a prominent Finnish physician. The book enjoyed such promotion and success that eventually one out of every 40 persons living in Finland had a copy of the book. A few years later, it was translated into Chinese and published in Singapore.

Harold's relationship with the *Youth's Instructor* spanned more than 35 years. His articles ranged from "Manners on Dates," "Some Husbands and Wives Stumble Over Pebbles," "True Love Is Patient," "Who Wants to Elope?" "How Bad Is Spinsterhood?" "Making Your Marriage Happier," "Symptoms Are Not Causes," "Nagging," and "One-Word Secret of Happiness," to "Words Are Powerful—Use Them Cautiously."

In time, the editors of *Signs of the Times, Life and Health,* and *These Times* magazines began accepting whatever Harold submitted. They forwarded questions from readers, which arrived in response to previous articles, and these served as the basis for future columns and articles.

At one time, after the American Medical Association published some of his articles in *Hygeia* for public consumption, Harold considered submitting articles to secular journals. But Daisy gently reminded him that "God's church comes first," and encouraged him to focus his writing talents on activities that carried eternal consequences for himself, his family, and his career ministries.

Some of Harold's most memorable counsel centered on family relationships. In "Save That Marriage" (*These Times,* April 1958), he outlined the basic causes of marital discord and some of the consequences of divorce.

> It is a delusion that divorce and remarriage offer a magic way to happiness. . . . The common complaint of "incompatibility," on which so many divorces are based, could in most cases, be correctly translated "selfishness," "intolerance," or "egotism." These are the basic faults which aggravate a mean temper or provoke the other symptoms that cause a husband and wife to think that they dislike each other. It is these basic faults that must be corrected if a couple in trouble are to save their marriage. If these go uncorrected, they will not only ruin the happiness of a first marriage but will keep a second marriage from being any better than the first.

Harold claimed that it's very natural for a person in difficulty to place more of the blame on the partner. And it's reasonable to assume that it would be easier to attain happiness with another person. "But," he told his readers, "the facts are that a person will carry his personal faults with him to a second marriage."

Shryock outlined the pitfalls of divorce and remarriage, including straining the financial resources from court costs, alimony, splitting property, and relocation. He included the disastrous consequences for a child.

> He may even become rebellious by refusing to believe that marriage can bring happiness. He may become resentful of the social order which, in his way of thinking, denied him a happy home such as other children have. This resentment easily takes the form of antisocial conduct.

Harold outlined the scriptural circumstances that allow for divorce.

> There are also good religious reasons for saving a marriage rather than taking recourse to divorce. The marriage vows constitute the most solemn kind of agreement that can be made by two human beings.

He indicated that in most cases of unhappiness between husbands and wives, the fault is two-sided.

> In one case it may appear that the husband is mostly to blame. In another case it may seem that the wife is most unreasonable. But usually both parties share in the blame. . . . But for the traits of selfishness, intolerance, and egotism, most troubles between husbands and wives could be avoided long before they reach critical proportions.

He concluded with "a magic fact of human relationship that can be used by either spouse to save a marriage." He claimed that it's something so simple that many couples overlook it. It sounds too good to be true and takes advantage of the fact that husbands and wives really do not want to break up their homes.

> To apply the magic, the specific accusations—nagging, indifference, temper, quarrelsomeness—must be ignored. Then, with courage born of a truly Christian outlook, the partner who determines to use the magic formula must first recognize his own personality weaknesses and acknowledge these to his partner. . . . His very admission of personal shortcomings will convince the other of his sincerity in desiring to preserve the marriage. What else can the partner do, then, but join in the program of correcting fundamental shortcomings in an all-out effort to save the marriage.

Shryock built the article around the experience of an actual couple who faced a difficult struggle. He gave examples of how the formula could work in their particular circumstance and concluded, "Magic? Really not—just common sense. But magic in the results that can be attained in saving a marriage—the most precious of all human relationships!"

⌒

Harold's writing career eventually evolved into a major undertaking, requiring considerable logistical support. The terms of his employment didn't provide secretarial help beyond what he needed for his administrative and teaching responsibilities. Harold never expected the medical school to provide secretarial assistance for his extracurricular activities. However, the volume of correspondence, requiring replies and the preparation of manuscripts for publication, required many hours of typing each week.

That's when Daisy rushed to the rescue. She'd turned from nursing to mothering at the end of World War II. But now, as her nest emptied, she volunteered to take charge of Harold's correspondence and the preparation of his many manuscripts. In grateful admiration, he borrowed the money to buy her a brand-new electric typewriter with which she could transcribe his recorded dictation and submit it to him for editing. And then she retyped the edited manuscript, making six copies at a time, almost error free.

Sometimes Daisy drove while Harold typed. A miscellaneous note in the January 1950 edition of *The [Alumni] Journal* provides a peek into the dynamics of the couple's dedication to CME, Harold's professional relationships, and his meticulous attention to detail:

> Dean Harold Shryock of Loma Linda is a man we can vote for as most likely to succeed in winning the hearts of the *Journal* staff. In the first place, he voluntarily sent us a report of the Interstate Postgraduate Assembly held in Philadelphia. Since volunteer reporters are as scarce as biddy molars, this deed alone won our hearts. In the second place, this busy dean listed all CME people who attended, giving them in alphabetical order, with complete and correctly spelled names, with class year, and with place of residence. "I am typing this while Daisy holds the car at 70 mph on a rolling highway through Kansas," he wrote. When we read this confession, we couldn't help wishing more Daisys would hold more cars at 70 mph while more Harolds whacked their typewriters.

During his writing career, Harold Shryock wrote 621 magazine articles in 16 publications for lay readers. Among them he wrote 196 articles for *Life and Health* magazine, 149 for *Signs of the Times,* 10 for *These Times,* 205 for the *Youth's Instructor,* seven for *Ministry,* 34 for the *Review and Herald,* and five for *Hygeia.* His versatility is evidenced by the fact that he also wrote the *Sabbath School Lesson Quarterly* for the third quarter of 1964.

Harold's words rolled off the presses at Pacific Press Publishing Association, Southern Publishing Association, Review and Herald Publishing Association, Malayan Signs Press, Norsk Bokforlag, Signes des Temps, Casa Editora Sudamericana, and Casa Publicadora Brasileira.

Harold's writing talent prompted Merlin Neff, book editor at Pacific Press, to track him down, in 1955, while he and Daisy were attending the East Pennsylvania camp meeting. "Dr. Shryock, I want you to expand your writing ministry into a new direction."

"How?"

"By succeeding Hubert O. Swartout, M.D. (CME: 1933), on the publication of *The New Modern Medical Counselor.* It's a one-volume medical book for lay people. As you may know, Swartout isn't in good health, and we need someone to carry on the project."

"Well, that's quite an opportunity," Harold responded. "Give me a little time to think."

Shryock had several reasons for being interested in the project. The Seventh-day Adventist Church first published a health book, written by John Harvey Kellogg, M.D., in 1877. It was called *The Household Manual of Hygiene.* To walk in the footsteps of such a pioneering author truly would be an honor. Also, Harold felt uniquely qualified to participate in such a project. He'd already successfully published articles and books on medical topics, all targeted to lay readers.

Upon returning home, Harold immediately contacted Swartout and found the ailing physician receptive to the idea. Succeeding another author in the writing of a book that's already underway isn't an easy assignment.

But before much could be done, Swartout's health began improving.

"I think I can continue with the manuscript," he told his editors.

That's when Neff had a bright idea. Since colporteurs were crying for books in two-volume sets, publishing advisers suggested expanding the project to include volumes emphasizing preventive medicine *plus* material on marriage and parenting. The two authors would simply divide the subjects. Swartout would update the material in his existing edition, and Shryock would prepare materials on the new topics.

"If two is good," Pacific Press reasoned, "then three would be even better!"

"Hold on, now," Harold responded. "This project is getting way too complicated. I may need to step aside."

"But, Dr. Shryock," the editors urged, "it's almost impossible to recruit a physician acquainted with medical literature and public health issues who also has the willingness to devote time to the job of producing a manuscript."

"That's exactly the problem," Harold told them. "I teach full time in the Department of Anatomy. My days and most nights are filled to overflowing as it is." He paused. "But, I do want to be involved with this project. I really do."

When the situation seemed hopeless, Harold remembered that he was entitled to a sabbatical year off. "I've got an idea," he told the editors at Pacific Press. "Why don't you hire me for one year and charge half of my salary to future royalties."

The only thing book editors love more than a good book is a good deal. Pacific Press quickly accepted the proposal and Shryock, freed from the pressures of his responsibilities at CME, completed his manuscript for the three-volume set during the next 12 months.

In this collection of books, Harold portrayed the human body as the handiwork of God, and presented disease as a consequence of violating heaven's laws of health. He stated repeatedly that the treatment of disease goes far beyond merely suppressing symptoms. "It's vitally important that we search for and remove the fundamental causes of disease—to prevent disease from occurring," he told readers.

Along with the entire writing, editing, and publishing team, Harold intended for the books to embody health education—to present to adult lay readers from all walks of life the health message foundation on which the Seventh-day Adventist denomination stands. Thirty-seven collaborators provided constructive criticism. Photographs and original art attractively illustrated each volume.

After all the 1970 edition had been sold, Harold became the sole author for the 1979 update. Because a private practice background was not the basis of his wisdom, he relied heavily on respected medical literature. Sources included the *Journal of the American Medical Association, The New England Journal of Medicine, The Harvard Medical School Newsletter,* and the vast resources of the Loma Linda University Library.

To keep track of his growing collection of medical material, he built a cupboard in his garage in which to store journals, and developed a system of organizing topics. Collaborators, faculty appointees from Loma Linda University School of Medicine—CME's successor—checked Harold's writings for accuracy. The volumes listed the names and professional status of these colleagues to demonstrate that the information presented was not based just on the author's opinion.

Preparing this second edition of the three-volume set kept Harold busy for many months after his retirement.

Because medical knowledge and understanding advance almost daily, the editors at Pacific Press proposed that Harold prepare a third edition of *You and Your Health* after he'd retired. "Now you'll have adequate time to thoroughly revise the medical set," they suggested.

Once again, his system of cross-referencing reliable medical journals worked perfectly and effectively.

For the 1985 edition Harold rearranged the chapters in all of the volumes and reorganized the general index to include new words that may be used by the lay public.

Somewhat as a courtesy, and also in recognition of the use of some of Harold's material from previous editions, Shryock was named coauthor of Dr. Mervyn Hardinge's 1991 edition of the series entitled *Family Medical Guide.*

~

Occasionally, in his dealings with church publishers, Harold experienced some of the unpleasant realities of the business world.

On one occasion, Harold won a $1,000 award in the health category of a writing contest for his book, *Mind If I Smoke?* The contest, sponsored by

Pacific Press, encouraged writers to contribute much-needed good literature. Shryock's up-to-date and authoritative work included 93 references from respected scientific sources. Merlin L. Neff, the book editor, congratulated Harold and predicted that the book would receive wide circulation. "Every young person in our denomination needs to have a book of this nature," he wrote in a personal letter to the author. "We are taking too much for granted with our young people today, thinking they are leaving alcohol and tobacco alone simply because the denomination frowns upon these destructive things."

The manager of the Pacific Press Book Department took a decidedly different view. "We can't be too optimistic," he told Harold, "because Adventists don't smoke." Harold had enough publishing experience to know that this lack of enthusiasm could affect the success of the book. He'd learned that books sell in direct proportion to the amount of marketing a publishing house utilizes.

Shryock had written the manuscript with the hope that it would be shared with smokers to awaken them to the dangers of their habit. The hazards of smoking were just beginning to be disseminated to the public.

Shryock quickly wrote back to Neff regarding the clearly conflicting predictions. As much as he appreciated the award, he emphasized that the book represented his long-range effort to get a message on smoking before many thousands of people—non-Adventists as well as Adventists. "This book wasn't written on the spur of the moment," he said. "It's been written thoughtfully from a file of material I've developed over a period of six years and from an active acquaintance with the current scientific literature. I'm writing in response to our church's practice of promoting healthful living and to help prevent disease and prolong life."

Also strongly motivating Shryock's letter to Neff was his conviction that cigarettes kill people and that tobacco companies were waging a very aggressive war of persuasion to portray smoking as an innocent pleasure to which people had a right. He saw the cigarette manufacturer's ad campaigns as an effort to diminish the public's newly developed uncertainty. *Mind If I Smoke?* represented Harold's one-man counterattack, and he felt confident that if one of the church's publishing houses refused to commit resources to this war, another would.

Shryock asked for an official commitment from the Press. "If this book is to receive wide circulation, I want to know when it will be published and how it will be promoted," he wrote. "But, if the book is not going to be promoted, I'll return the award and ask that my manuscript, and the rights to its publication, be returned as well. Then I'll seek a publisher who shares my belief that this book should run many thousands of impressions and be actively and aggressively promoted."

He ended his letter by stating, "I believe . . . that it is better to settle the matter by a frank approach at this juncture than to wish, later, that we had had a clearer understanding."

While most authors would have been thrilled to have a book accepted by a major denominational publishing house, to Harold, it was nothing new. Most writers would have pocketed the $1,000 and hoped for the best. But not this writer. In the interest of serving as many as possible in the church and in secular society—he was fighting for a cause. He knew beyond a doubt that tobacco was the most devastating drug on the planet, affecting millions of lives. He hadn't researched and written the book just to let it sit and gather dust in some editor's file cabinet or watch it languish, unheralded, in the bargain bin of Adventist bookstores.

Neff responded appropriately and with well-deserved concern. "I deeply appreciate your frankness," he wrote, "for it may help to clarify some matters that have been burdening us for some time." He went on to criticize his own book department for its lack of vision. "I think our management is quite worked up over the matter now, and I expect to see some good results."

Neff also stated that his original letter of optimism reflected management's view, and that the book was already being edited. In addition, the statistical information would be dramatized with graphs or other visual aids, and the book would be in production within two weeks. He acknowledged the timeliness of Shryock's manuscript, adding that his colleagues were anxious to get the book into print as soon as possible; and he mentioned that one of the review judges, a physician, had reported that the work was the finest he'd read in years.

"I think you have lighted the match to a fire that will make some things hot around here," he concluded. "We shall endeavor to throw our advertising and publicity behind it and get the very best cooperation from the various departments in this monumental piece of work, such as we have not had before in any of our literature."

In time, Pacific Press came through on its promises, successfully publishing *Mind If I Smoke?* in cloth and paper bindings through three revisions. By May 1968 it had sold more than 100,000 copies and began appearing in barber shops, beauty salons, libraries (high schools, colleges and cities), and in physician's and dentist's offices.

In 1981 Pacific Press replaced it with Shryock's new book, *We've Come a Long Way—Maybe.* This volume emphasized how to quit smoking and the wisdom of never starting.

Today, an impressive list of Shryock's publications testifies to the man's amazing productivity within this avocational pursuit, each enhanced by his professional expertise. Becoming an author combined Harold's interests in counseling, medicine, psychology, and teaching.

When he started writing in the ninth grade to impress and entertain his composition teacher, Providence was laying the foundation for a future international ministry through the written word.

Chapter 13

Third and Fourth Callings?

arold Shryock's reputation as an accomplished author, along with his faculty position at CME and his experiences as a student of psychology, made him a much sought-after counselor and public speaker. Students at the schools he visited especially appreciated that someone on the CME faculty would listen to their concerns.

Harold also counseled relatives of students and institution employees. His clientele included medical professionals who sought his advice years after sitting in his classes. Empathy and compassion, born of his own personal struggles, pervaded Harold's counseling ministry. Sometimes painful events in his own life added insights he wouldn't have gained otherwise.

In 1957, a new ministry developed when *Youth's Instructor* editor Walter Crandall extended yet another challenge. "The need for translating Seventh-day Adventist ideals into the circumstances and problems of modern living is one of the top-priority needs for the young people of the church," he wrote in a letter to Harold.

To address these concerns, Shryock appealed to readers of the *Youth's Instructor* to propose topics for discussion. Suggestions, inquiries, and requests for counsel came from around the world. Many young people poured out their hearts and souls, attempting to find solutions to their perplexing personal circumstances.

Daisy's long hours at the typewriter made it possible for Harold to respond. A file of source material developed out of the correspondence consisting of the readers' longings, quandaries, and heartaches. There was no longer a question of where Harold would get material for his next column.

It now became a matter of choosing among the many urgent problems entrusted to him.

⌒

Harold's counseling ministry to young people eventually became his focus. Although he'd not been trained as such, his professional experience in teaching psychology and in studying psychiatry, combined with decades of active counseling, led him to publish a two-part series in *Ministry* magazine during the late 1960s. In "The Minister as a Marriage Counselor," he shared valuable insights.

He called counseling "a privilege and rewarding experience," with the most favorable results obtained during an informally conducted interview. He outlined how to avoid professional risks, warned against issuing mandates, and encouraged his minister-readers to guide their clients into clarifying their own issues before participating in the development of their own solutions. He admitted that, in some instances, it would be better to refer the client to another counselor, physician, or attorney. "Allow your clients to feel their emotions as a normal response to facing difficulties."

Then Harold underscored the importance of confidentiality. "The only safe course is not to mention the contents of your counseling interviews to anyone, not even your wife or fellow minister."

He opened and closed the article by emphasizing the importance of spirituality, urging his readers to conclude each counseling session with prayer. Inspired years earlier by nurse Frank (Monty) Montgomery, a conversation with God always closed Harold's conversation with a searching soul. Because of his broad contacts with Adventist youth, Harold Shryock was invited to speak at a number of youth congresses and camp meetings across the country.

⌒

After Patti and Ed flew from the nest, Harold and Daisy often took to the road together. They experienced their most exciting and memorable trip between the camp meetings in Pugwash, Nova Scotia, and St. Johns, Newfoundland.

St. Johns physician and former student of Harold, Eugene W. Hildebrand, M.D. (CME: 1953-B), an ex-navigator on a World War II bomber that had survived 50 missions over Germany, warned the couple that they should make the trip by air instead of train. Shryock had always shown deference to Daisy's fear of flying. But Newfoundland was still quite remote and the only way to get to some villages was by air, boat, or train. "Train schedules are unreliable," Hildebrand declared, "and your locomotive might hit a moose or get derailed. You really should fly."

He promised to meet the Shryocks in Gander, Newfoundland, a refueling station for transcontinental flights, and then drive them to St. Johns. Taking the advice to heart, Harold quickly booked one-way passage on Canadian Airways for himself and his apprehensive wife.

Fog held the 7:00 a.m. flight on the tarmac until just past noon. When they finally got into the air, the journey proved most enjoyable. The two sat with their noses pressed against the cool window, as a rugged and breathtaking landscape slipped by under them.

As promised, Hildebrand and family met the late-arriving Shryocks and then loaded them into his brand-new Chevrolet for the trip to St. Johns. The last section of the Trans Canada Highway to St. Johns was still under construction and proved quite bumpy. Harold soon grew to appreciate Hildebrand's brand of driving. The doctor raced over the unfinished road at top speed, apparently concluding that the laws of physics would keep him floating along the tops of the rocks and missing all the bumps in between.

The large Seventh-day Adventist Church in St. Johns, where the camp meeting was being held, accommodated 300 people from all over the province, including three General Conference appointees. At the end of the sessions, many church folk came to say goodbye to the church dignitaries and the Shryocks at the train depot. Due to scheduling difficulties, a return flight was not an option. The group faced a 600-mile trip to Nova Scotia—the last 100 miles on an ocean ferry.

The next morning the train roared into Corner Brook, Newfoundland, a main rail connection, and quickly changed crews. Soon it was on its way again, but quickly came to a bone-jarring, screeching halt.

Harold stumbled out of the bathroom, toothbrush in hand, just as the brakeman appeared in the passageway. "You're a doctor, right?" he called.

"Yes."

"Good. We either hit a moose or we're off the track, and some of our passengers might be injured. Please come with me."

After checking to make sure that Daisy was OK, Harold disappeared out the door, following on the heels of the worried rail worker.

They found the two diesel engines, still sitting on the narrow-gauge track ahead. But the full-size, top-heavy, American-made railcars following them failed to negotiate a curve, uncoupled from the engines, and left the track. The baggage car traveled a considerable distance into the trees. The self-guided transports ripped down telephone lines and one tipped over onto its side.

Quickly, Harold climbed inside the overturned car only to find that, thankfully, all the passengers had already escaped.

Functioning as doctor and nurse, the Shryocks, accompanied by the brakeman, examined the frightened, mud-stained people moving about in a shock-induced daze. No one had been killed, but several had been injured. They sent back two of the more critically injured passengers, on a small handcar, to the previous town for treatment.

The wreckage had torn up the tracks, making the area impassable. Two other trains arrived late that afternoon, stopping on opposite ends of the carnage. The Shryocks and other passengers dug through the debris to find their luggage, then boarded the train headed for Port aux Basques, where they hoped to continue their journey on the ferry.

The train finally puffed into the port city about midnight in the middle of a heavy downpour. The ferry scheduled to take them the last 100 miles had already departed.

"This day just can't get any worse!" Harold moaned to his tired wife.

He was wrong.

The late-arriving passengers caught a ride on an icebreaker that was not equipped to transport passengers; it had few accommodations and absolutely no food. The Shryocks found a berth in the hold of the ship and tried their best to settle in to catch some sleep.

Next morning, Harold started to get up, but quickly found that his constitution was way out of harmony with the unpredictable movement of the ocean. To say he was seasick would be a gross understatement.

The doctor looked around, weaving like a drunken man. "Daisy?" he called, trying his best to control his gurgling stomach. "Daisy? Where are you?"

He eventually found her up on deck . . . bird-watching.

After returning to Loma Linda, the Shryocks received a letter from the railroad company thanking them for their assistance. Daisy concluded that maybe flying wasn't all that bad after all.

⌒

Harold's speaking engagements kept him on the road constantly, traveling from one end of the nation to the other, speaking on the timeless themes of love, courtship, and marriage.

Harold was guest speaker at faculty retreats, teachers' conventions, academy and college chapel services, colporteur institutes, and Missionary Volunteer Society rallies. He also stood before numerous high school and college classes and medical-ministerial convocations.

In his public speaking, as in his teaching, writing, and counseling, he always focused his efforts on making the subject of the day relevant to his listeners.

His calendar recorded speaking appointments at home and school and parent-teacher association meetings in 16 Southern California cities from San Diego to Ventura and points inland. He conducted weeks of prayer at academies and colleges from California to Tennessee.

Harold preached sermons in 21 churches across California, and at Thunderbird Academy near Phoenix, Arizona, and Southern Missionary College [now Southern Adventist University] in Tennessee. He spoke at CME/LLU alumni meetings and youth congresses across the United States.

Harold always considered it a privilege, and a tremendous responsibility, to appeal to Adventist youth to uphold Christian ideals in social conduct. He felt that the hand of Providence had placed him at the crossroads of the denomination. With the Lord's help he used his energies to direct the minds of Adventist youth to the principles of true love and purity enunciated by the Great Physician. The spiritual and social impact of Harold Shryock's life cannot be measured.

Chapter 14

Family Fun and a Big Scare

As Patti and husband Carleton's family grew to include three daughters, proud grandparents Harold and Daisy often took the group camping to Borrego Springs, California. During these trips, Harold would load the excited, energetic Wallace girls on his bicycle and head off for a ride through the countryside—one balancing on the bar in front of him, one standing on a rack behind him, and one sitting on his shoulders—all three children smiling broadly and squealing happily as the warm wind whistled through their hair.

After years as avid outdoor campers, the Shryocks traded in their cots, sleeping bags, and family tents for a 16-foot camping trailer. The Wallaces slept in their station wagon while their three offspring drifted into dreamland tucked snuggly in special beds Harold built for them in the trailer.

Harold and Daisy, often camped with their granddaughters for three weeks at a time as far north as Canada. The Shryock family agrees that Harold adored Daisy and that the Shryocks had a wonderful marriage. But that didn't mean they didn't have occasional disagreements. Once, when the Shryocks camped with their granddaughters near Lake Louise, the girls witnessed one of these events. Harold said, "I didn't say that, Lover."

Daisy responded, "Yes you did, Lover."

Then Harold concluded, "You can just go jump in the lake, Lover." But these disagreements were short-lived. The campers rode bicycles together and studied flowers, berries, and birds. On such occasions, Harold happily pursued his nature photography hobby.

Daisy loved birding and Harold loved her for it. She eventually added more than 600 different species to her lifetime list. Harold understood that, in order for birders to discover that new and rare species, they had to go where the birds were. He reveled in the pleasure of taking his wife to wild places where hawks, ducks, and song birds gather, becoming her eager chauffeur and enjoying their many walks together through dark, quiet woodlands and sun-drenched meadows.

Birding took place right in the couple's back yard, too. The Shryocks set up a feeder where they watched mockingbirds, red-winged blackbirds, hummingbirds, scrub jays, and even crows devour the seeds they supplied. Harold admitted that the scrub jay caused his systolic blood pressure to jump five points. Its pattern and coloring matched almost exactly the unique blue and gray uniform worn by the New Jersey highway patrolman who pulled him over just, Shryock insisted, because he drove like a Californian.

One of the couple's birding expeditions led to the gratifying discovery that a CME graduate and his wife were building a unique ministry.

Harold and Daisy traveled to Patagonia, Arizona—a small farming community 20 miles from the border of Mexico. Patagonia, the home of a 500-acre conservancy that operated a bird sanctuary, boasted only one main and one side-street. A popular venue for bird lovers, the town and surrounding farms maintained a human population of about 200.

Harold decided to pay a visit to Delmar R. Mock, M.D. (CME class of 1946), who was practicing in Patagonia. When he asked an attendant at the local service station if he knew the physician, the attendant responded with a smile, "Oh sure. I know Dr. Mock. But he ain't here. He left town earlier this morning to see patients in a nearby village."

The attendant directed the Shryocks to Dr. Mock's home on the side street across from a small church. A hospitable Mrs. Mock greeted the visitors and warmly invited them in. After bringing them up to date on their many projects, the lady of the house led the couple down a hallway and opened a door into a one-room school where 25 students sat before one teacher.

Years before, Dr. and Mrs. Mock had adopted Patagonia, Arizona, as their personal mission field. They'd funded the little school and built the modest church across the street. Dr. Mock served as the lone country doctor, sometimes making house calls 50 to 60 miles away within his 2,500-square-mile practice. In the midst of their birding trip, the Shryocks enjoyed the happy and surprising discovery that a former CME student and his wife were putting to work the evangelistic tools they'd studied at medical school.

Harold enjoyed Daisy's avocation as a birder because it provided pleasant companionship with his wife and also threw open a window into the mysteries of creation and God's participation in the minutiae of life. This latter reason held special importance to the physician-teacher. He'd enjoyed abundant evidence of God's participation in his life. Although there'd been times when he'd step back emotionally and regroup, he always considered the twists and turns to be providential.

During his ministry, he often called people's attention to God's leading, sharing with them his own experiences with his heavenly Father. Even his diverse extra-curricular activities he accepted as divine callings, enabling him to minister to untold thousands. Through it all, Daisy stood firmly by his side, administering large doses of love and encouragement right when he needed it most.

In 1984 Daisy developed some troubling symptoms involving dizziness and a loss of muscular control in her extremities. She began dropping dishes and developed a peculiar gait. Consulting specialists diagnosed Daisy's problem as a compression of the spinal cord in the cervical region of her neck. Because she suffered from mild osteoarthritis, they assumed that osteophytes were compressing her spinal cord, a condition with no cure.

The couple turned to neurosurgeon Robert S. Knighton, M.D., Shryock's former model-making student whom he'd taken to neurology clinics in Los Angles 47 years before. Knighton had recently retired in nearby Cherry Valley and had accepted a temporary position as chief of the Division of Neurosurgery while the Loma Linda University School of Medicine looked for a permanent replacement.

Knighton became the consultant on the case and agreed with the neurologists that pressure caused by osteophytes was the most probable cause of Daisy's symptoms. But then he surprised everyone by adding, "But it could be a meningioma that's compressing the spinal cord and causing the problems." Harold knew that a meningioma was a benign tumor in the tissues surrounding the spinal cord. If his former student was correct, the offending growth could be removed.

The doctor recommended a myelogram to determine whether Daisy's condition was in fact the result of such a tumor. Daisy resisted, knowing that the procedure carried with it serious risks. But, after the Christmas and New Year's holidays had passed, her symptoms increased to such an extent that she began dragging one foot when walking. "I'll follow Dr. Knighton's suggestion," she announced, resigning herself to its outcome— whatever that might be.

A myelogram was quickly scheduled. After studying the results, both Knighton and Harold hurried to Daisy's room to tell her the good news. It *was* a meningioma! If the benign tumor was removed surgically, her prospect for recovery was good.

Knighton had lost none of the precision skills he'd demonstrated decades earlier in Harold's laboratory. His three-hour surgery completely removed the rare tumor, but a question remained. How much permanent damage had already occurred? How much recovery of function was possible? Daisy underwent several weeks of rehabilitation after she returned home. Progress was slow, but within a matter of months she'd recovered most of the function she'd lost. Harold's belief that his talented student would someday become a great blessing to humanity came full-circle.

The Shryocks' and Knighton's respect and appreciation was mutual. In later years, Knighton told a gathering of physicians, "I can say that, in my opinion, Dr. Shryock is the finest teacher I ever encountered, but also the most kind and gentle human being; and I am very grateful for having been associated with him."

Chapter 15

Reflections on a Life

arold Shryock retired as professor of anatomy on August 31, 1975, after 41 years of service. He received a letter of appreciation from Dr. V. Norskov Olsen, president of Loma Linda University, announcing that the board of trustees had voted to appoint him emeritus professor of anatomy, effective November 1, 1975.

On November 16, 1976, Raymond O. West, M.D. (CME: 1952), added his own expression of respect:

> I shall never forget my gratitude to you for having given me the opportunity to become a physician in the first place. Then there was your teaching, and I dare say that, while you may have had your peers, I have not sat at the feet of a finer teacher and learned from him words of life and truth. You were one of the very few who stood on the summit when in the classroom. . . .
>
> Then there was your consistent Christian life, an influence that must have affected favorably all who came within your sphere of influence. . . . The Medical School and the University have been better because of your presence; and, for many of us, Heaven is more likely because of your life.

Harold appreciated such words of gratitude and found ways to encourage others even in response to his own retirement. To a group of medical students he wrote:

> Life involves many transitions. Eventually there comes the

unavoidable transition from active professional life to retirement. Thus far I have enjoyed all the transitions, and I expect to enjoy this one, too. But there is yet one more transition that we Christians anticipate most hopefully, and this will be the most significant of all. Let us all share this expectation.

I have enjoyed my career as a teacher and would not want to do otherwise even if I could live life over again. Two major factors have contributed to this enjoyment: (1) my wife's willingness and sympathetic encouragement for me to follow the career of my preference, regardless of monetary considerations; and (2) the stimulating experience of matching wits with students.

For me, teaching has been an interesting career because it has answered the question: Can the Lord take a person with handicaps and personal defects and make him useful?

Being active in the production of book manuscripts cushioned Harold's adjustment to retirement. He and Daisy worked together as a team. He considered her to be a favorably prejudiced critic. She was his life partner in everything.

Because of Harold's long association with the institution, he was often asked to speak to new students. In August 1986, he presented an eloquent testimony to a group of freshman medical students regarding the providential timing and other divine influences that blessed the institution's perilous beginning. He concluded with a tribute to his late father, who'd passed away in 1950, and unveiled a watercolor portrait of Alfred by his former student, Joseph Mossberger, a retired pathologist. Harold introduced the artist by saying:

> Dr. Mossberger retained his interest in art. And even though now handicapped by poor health, he's had opportunity to look back on his career and remember the teacher who gave him encouragement when he was a freshmen and sophomore. . . . He considers him almost like a father—a mentor. And so he has chosen . . . as a subject of his crowning masterpiece, my father's face.

Pausing, and visibly overcome with emotion, Harold was unsuccessful in his attempt to maintain his composure.

> I've already seen [this masterpiece]. . . . It did something to me. . . . It was an emotional experience. My father has been dead for 38 years, but it brought him to life in my thinking.

Remembering his father's lifelong influence, he added,

> [Dad] spoke to me. He said, "Harold . . . do your best. Harold . . . I'm always on your side. Harold . . . don't forget you are here for a purpose."
>
> In a few moments you will see this masterpiece unveiled. If you will . . . it will speak to you. . . . You will see it from day to day as you come and go. It will say to you, if you will, "John . . . Mary . . . do your best. Remember that the institution in which you are was of divine timing. Remember that there are many who would like to be where you are now. Remember that this privilege of yours carries an obligation to fulfill the divine purpose for which you were brought to this place in life.

Pam Bishop, one of Harold's granddaughters, paid a tribute to him at his and Daisy's sixtieth wedding anniversary on April 30, 1989. She acknowledged that he'd given her two of the three special things she loved looking at in their home: a china cake plate and an antique rocker, which she put to use with her own three children. She continued by saying that she did not yet have the third special thing: a picture of Jesus painted by a former student and given to Harold's father as a token of his gratitude. Then Pam paused, adding:

> Or, do I? Was it Jesus I saw in Gramps that night he picked me up off the pavement, doctored my bleeding knee, and took me to 31 Flavors for a triple cone? Was it He who spoke all those words of encouragement, faith, and love through these years, the One who upheld the standard of patience, longsuffering, and grace?

Harold expressed his love for his family in different ways throughout the rest of his life. For example, when his granddaughters were in college, he followed them from Loma Linda for 30 miles to Corona, honked his horn after he determined that they had arrived home safely, and then returned to Loma Linda.

Sweet, lively, affectionate, and supportive Daisy eventually declined physically as the years went by, a victim of Ménière's disease, an irritation of the inner ear resulting in total deafness. On May 18, 1992, she suffered a stroke and died.

Harold and Daisy had been happily married for 63 years and, according to members of the family, never lost their romantic spark. With a ready smile on her face and a twinkle in her eye, Daisy spent her adult life providing balance to Harold's decision-making and problem-solving activities. Without her by his side, he never could have accomplished so much for so long.

Although living alone for almost 12 years, Harold Shryock still enjoyed his family. He was an inspiration, a positive energy, and a great encourager. He especially enjoyed amusing his eight grandchildren and nine great-grandchildren, who adored him.

To inspire levity and spontaneity when family pictures were taken, Harold made faces and noises, including a horselaugh. He puffed out his cheeks and shook his head so fast that his cheeks flew "all over the place." Then he was urged to continue. "Do your cheeks, Grandpa," the children begged. "Do your cheeks."

He loved to get the details right, as illustrated by his remembrance of birthdays. Harold's greetings arrived on time, every time, and included the loved one's birth date and an appropriate, handwritten, personal message. He was greatly esteemed as the family patriarch.

On April 14, 1996, the Shryock family celebrated Harold's 90th birthday. Everyone was there—his two children and two foster children, Helen (Daisy's "sister"), and all of his grandchildren and great-grandchildren. Ed spoke in his father's honor:

On this wonderful occasion we come together for the purpose of marking and celebrating a very important milestone that has been achieved by the one [who represents] a very important influence in all our lives.

We have all been touched as we have all taken notice and made adjustments in our own lives because of his influence. Influence is important when it helps us stay on course or when it causes us to make corrections and decisions in our lives which will ultimately assist us in achieving the goal of eternity. . . . The influence of a good and righteous man makes those who observe this life have thoughts about their own life and their own objectives. . . . If you've ever been in a harbor and observed a well-known ship that has seen it all, taken the trips to battle, endured the worst from enemy and storm, and brought the troops back home, there's something very awesome about that ship, docked there in silence.

There's something about a good example, a successful mission that makes you want to follow. . . . We are all here today . . . because we want to honor someone who has made a big difference. . . .

At this point, Ed became visibly overcome with emotion. After 15 long seconds of silence, during which he glanced at his father, he said to the group, "You'll have to excuse me." Another 10 seconds later, after regaining his composure, he continued.

. . . has made a big difference in our lives. We want to say thank you for being who you are, for standing up for what you believe, and for giving us an example worthy of following. . . . I can't speak for everyone that's here today, but I can speak for myself from personal experience.

There was another eight-second pause. Then Ed asked out loud "Why did I write this like this?" The family chuckled.

Dad, your example has helped me make decisions that I probably would not have made if you had not been the person you are.

Patti then shared some of her experiences, including one of Harold's methods of teaching her financial responsibility.

> He started me out on a bank account when I went away to college and said, "This is a good time for you to learn how to budget. So I'll give you so much a month, and if you run over your budget, then you have to earn it and pay the rest of it off." Well, I thank him today for that. I was 17 and . . .

Just then Carleton interrupted and said, "I thank you for that too, Dad."

For years, following visits to his family, Harold's lifelong love affair with the automobile contributed to a unique way of saying goodbye. Instead of waving his hand, flashing his lights, or tooting his horn, Harold laid a strip of Michelin rubber, often at the encouragement of his grandchildren. "Speed off, Grandpa," they'd shout. Harold obliged by depressing the brake pedal with his left foot, mashing the accelerator with his right foot, and then releasing the brake. The resulting high-frequency squeal could be heard for blocks.

Harold's chariot of choice—a low-mileage, silver, 1985 Ford Crown Victoria—was hardly considered a muscle car. But in Harold Shryock's hands. . . . Shryock drove his chariot furiously, even in his 90s. When he turned 92, his family persuaded him to restrain himself and discontinue his dramatic departures. They also convinced his younger relatives to stop egging him on.

Responding to a debilitating illness Harold suffered in April 1999, Patti relieved her father of his car keys, gave them to Ed, and indicated that they'd be returned when everyone felt it was safe for the family patriarch to resume driving. A few days later Harold needed a haircut. He simply whipped out his spare set of keys and smugly moseyed downtown to Frank's Barbershop.

In January 2000, Harold moved into Linda Valley Villa, a retirement center within sight of where the Loma Linda depot once welcomed him and his parents on January 1, 1910. The Villa provided good meals and good neighbors, including longtime friends, former colleagues, and even some of his former dietetics students.

In reminiscing, Harold admitted he wished he could have learned earlier the importance of being more friendly, congenial, and tolerant. Harold did acknowledge that his parents' over-dominance handicapped him in his adolescent adjustments. Nevertheless, he recognized that their motives were good, and that they eventually made considerable sacrifices on his behalf. Furthermore, in spite of his parents' efforts to direct his life, he felt that his father was totally unselfish in his deep interest in his son's progress. Harold cherished his father's influence.

Fortunately, just before Alfred Shryock died, he confided to Daisy his deep remorse for the way she'd been treated. Daisy appreciated his sincere and straightforward apology and told him so.

Looking back over almost a hundred years of life, Harold advised young people to safeguard their health and obtain the best education possible. "Accept and cultivate worthy ideals," he urged, "and trust in God."

As a teenager and young adult with handicaps to overcome, he felt insecure and doubted he could make a success of his life. But, with the passing of time, he learned to trust in God's providential interventions. Throughout the years, he often saw God's influences.

Although his story is the story of one man, the man reveals the leading of Providence. Harold refused to take credit for any of the marvelous events that highlighted his years. "I was merely a bystander as Providence blessed the institution," he wrote to Dr. B. Lyn Behrens, president of Loma Linda University Adventist Health Sciences Center.

Providence armed Harold with great strength and inspiration over decades of challenges and uncertainties. He believed that God's influences had blessed and will continue to bless the institution he loved. "We must avoid being smug about our present, praiseworthy circumstances," he wrote in the March-April, 1991 issue of *The [Alumni] Journal.* He added:

> Our history reveals that it is the Lord's blessing and overruling Providence that has brought us to where we are. . . . We of the present generation are now reaping, by way of the Lord's blessing, the benefits of the faith and devotion of those who established and maintained the institution in its early years. Let us not take credit to ourselves for the institution's good name and

worthy accomplishments. Rather, we need to pray humbly for divine guidance that the institution may continue to fulfill the Lord's purpose.

In 1910, as a very young Harold Shryock disembarked with his parents from the railroad train at the Loma Linda station, the boy could not have imagined that someday he'd play a major role in the development of a world-renowned institution. He couldn't have foreseen an organization that produced tens of thousands of alumni—men and women who've been trained to bring healing to body, mind, and soul.

Harold Shryock received great satisfaction from his contribution to the cause of God, by proxy, through his former students. In addition to Robert S. Knighton and Delmar R. Mock, others symbolize the quantity, quality, and variety of contributions made by those who once sat at his feet.

- David B. Hinshaw, M.D. (CME: 1947), known as a man of vision, became chair of the Department of Surgery. He took on the responsibility of dean of the School of Medicine in 1962, a position he held for 13 years. Hinshaw's implementation of the board of trustees' decision to consolidate the School of Medicine in Loma Linda, resulting in the construction of Loma Linda University Medical Center, is a testimony to his leadership.

- Edward H. Hon, M.D. (CME: 1950), with an extensive background in electronics engineering, developed the world's first fetal monitoring system. In a feature story in 1969, Life magazine projected that Hon's system could save as many as 20,000 babies a year.

- David J. Baylink, M.D., F.A.C.B. (CME: 1957), is presently a distinguished professor of medicine at Loma Linda University and associate vice president for medical affairs for research and director of the Musculoskeletal Disease Center at the Jerry L. Pettis Memorial Veterans Medical Center in Loma Linda. Baylink is one of the world's leading authorities on osteoporosis, a prevalent and costly disease among the elderly. He has received many awards for his work on bone and mineral metabolism, including the Medical Investigator Award, Veterans Administration; he has published over 500 scholarly papers in the musculoskeletal field, including molecular genetics, tissue regeneration, and gene therapy.

☞ Stanley G. Sturges, M.D. (CME: 1955), became "Mr. America" to a superstitious people who lived in one of the most isolated spots in the world. He built the 22-bed Scheer Memorial Hospital in Banepa, Nepal, in the midst of the Himalayas—without the use of modern tools. Not even a wheelbarrow. In 1961, during an event that garnered national press, radio, and television coverage, the 6-foot 4-inch Sturges received the United States Junior Chamber of Commerce's Award as one of America's Ten Outstanding Young Men. Sturges' wife, Raylene Duncan Sturges, R.N, a 1953 graduate of the CME School of Nursing, became the little hospital's "doctor" when her husband treated patients at distant Nepalese villages. Raylene and Patti Shryock had been high school friends.

☞ Edwin H. Krick, M.D. (CME: 1961), became a medical missionary to Japan, where he became one of the few Western physicians to write and pass the Japanese Medical Board examinations in Japanese. He practiced medicine in Tokyo and Kobe. In 1973 he reestablished the Kobe Adventist Hospital, the first denominationally operated hospital in the Far East, which opened its doors in 1902. It has since grown from 45 to 116 beds. He eventually returned to Loma Linda and became chief of the division of rheumatology in the School of Medicine and head of the division of preventive medicine. Between 1986 and 1990, he was dean of the School of Public Health.

☞ Melvin P. Judkins, M.D. (CME: 1947), developed, in 1966, the Judkins Technique of Selective Coronary Arteriography—the most widely used technique in the world for X-ray evaluations of the blood vessels of the heart. Without the definitive information provided by the procedure, balloon angioplasty and coronary bypass surgery, which offer relief of pain and extend life to many heart patients, would not be possible.

☞ Eugene W. Hildebrand, M.D. (CME: 1953), is the physician who took Harold and Daisy from Gander, Newfoundland, to a camp meeting in St. Johns in 1959. During that camp meeting, Hildebrand borrowed a financially challenged schoolteacher's car and returned it with four new tires. He delivered 300 babies a year during his 10 years in Newfoundland. Then he served as a medical missionary for various lengths of time in Libya, South Vietnam, Loma Linda, Alaska, the Dominican Republic, Palau, the Marshall Islands, and Indonesia. Shryock was deeply pleased that Hildebrand used the education and inspiration he received at CME to turn bombing missions into medical missions in the service of mankind. And the admiration was mutual. Hildebrand and his wife, Jean, named their youngest son Harold in recognition of Eugene's high regard for Shryock.

- James M. Slater, M.D. (CME: 1963), and the Loma Linda University Medical Center opened the world's first hospital-based Proton Treatment Center in October 1990. The $100 million facility includes a proton accelerator and three-story proton guidance system that weighs 400 tons and produces up to 250 million electron volts of radiation. It's now being used to treat cancer and other diseases with far more precision than would be possible with conventional radiation. The facility has been in full operation since the summer of 1994 and is capable of serving up to 200 patients a day. Headed by Slater, the project to build the facility was an international effort to benefit mankind and involved up to 120 scientists from high-energy physics research laboratories around the world. Through NASA research, it is contributing to the safety of those living in the International Space Station.

- G. Gordon Hadley, M.D. (CME: 1944-B), a pathologist, served as a missionary to the Christian Medical College in Vellore, India. He became the first American to teach at the University of Kabul, Afghanistan—and was still teaching there at age 82. He accepted the role of dean of the Loma Linda University School of Medicine from 1977 to 1986. He was medical secretary of the Health and Temperance Department for the General Conference of Seventh-day Adventists from 1985 to 1990; he then became president of the 15-story, 400-bed Sir Run Run Shaw Hospital in Hangzhou, China, for more than six and one half years. Sir Run Run Shaw, a Chinese philanthropist, funded most of the hospital with the understanding that the Seventh-day Adventist Church and Loma Linda University and Medical Center would be involved in its planning and implementation.

☞ James G. Haughton, M.D. (CME: 1950), M.P.H., served the New York inner city as executive medical director of the Department of Public Health and the first deputy commissioner of New York City hospitals. He eventually became the chief deputy of Health Services Administration in New York. Over the years, he joined the faculties of Yale University, University of Michigan, Roosevelt University, Carnegie Mellon University of Medical Science, Northwestern University, Drew University of Medicine and Science, and Columbia University. He became chief executive officer of the Health and Hospitals Governing Commission of Cook County, Illinois, and vice president of Drew University. He then was named director of the Department of Health and Human Services in the City of Houston and medical director of King/Drew Medical Center in Los Angeles. Haughton is presently medical director of public health for Los Angeles County.

☞ Ivan M. Angell, M.D. (CME: 1950), lived for a while in a cardboard box in an orange grove following the divorce of his parents when he was 8. He eventually became a teacher and then entered CME at age 39. He served for 28 years at Bella Vista Hospital in Puerto Rico and then helped establish a hospital in Haiti, one of the most poverty-stricken and needy countries on earth. After his retirement, at age 72, he continued to provide relief for missionary physicians in Monument Valley, Utah; Cambodia; and Thailand.

☞ C. Joan Coggin, M.D. (CME: 1953-A), a cardiologist, cofounded the Loma Linda University Overseas Heart Surgery Team in 1963. The team has performed heart surgeries in more countries than any other similar organization. Members not only perform surgery, but also teach local professionals the technical skills and teamwork necessary to equal the success found in the best surgery centers in the United States. Coggin, recently retired as vice president for global outreach for Loma Linda University Adventist Health Sciences Center.

☞ Lawrence D. Longo, M.D. (CME: 1954), is a distinguished professor of physiology and of obstetrics and gynecology at Loma Linda University. For many years, Longo has explored various aspects of the dynamics and regulation of respiratory gas exchanges in the placenta and oxygenation of the fetus. In conjunction with these studies, Longo wrote the section in the U.S. Surgeon General's Report on smoking and health hazards to the mother and fetus. He also played a key role in legislation requiring warning labels on cigarette packages regarding the hazards of smoking in relation to heart disease, lung disease, and problems for the pregnant woman and her fetus. Longo has served as a scientific consultant to the National Institutes of Health, National Science Foundation, and National Research Council. He also serves on an advisory panel of the Environmental Protection Agency, which made recommendations leading to enactment of the Clean Air Act. During the past decade, Longo has concentrated his effort on understanding basic biochemical mechanisms of signal transduction in cerebral arteries, and their change with development. He works to apply this scientific knowledge to improving bedside management of premature infants with problems of blood flow in the brain, so complications such as cerebral palsy, mental retardation, and related disorders can be prevented. Longo has published papers on various aspects of the history of obstetrics and gynecology, particularly during the eighteenth and nineteenth centuries. He has authored more than 300 scientific papers and nine books, and his research has been funded by the National Institutes of Health and other agencies for almost four decades.

☞ Earl C. Mercill, M.D. (CME: 1950), along with his wife Mariane, a 1949 graduate of the CME School of Nursing, chose to meet the urgent medical needs of an isolated, low-income logging community in Northern California. Hayfork, near Weaverville and Deadman's Gulch, is halfway between Redding and the Pacific Ocean. There, Mercill labored as the town's only physician for 35 of his 51-year career. He treated colds and disease, sewed up cuts, made house calls, delivered babies—sometimes by lantern and flashlight—and endeared himself as the town's self-sacrificing, often unpaid "Doc." He responded to serious logging accidents deep in the woods and, seeing to the community's needs, even sewed up injured animals, including horses. After retirement, Mercill continued seeing patients and making house calls. In addition to their four children, the Mercill's reared four adopted and foster children "simply because the kids needed a mother and a daddy and brothers and sisters." Even their private life became a ministry.

All these men and women, representing hundreds of Harold Shryock's former students, can certainly be called "unsung heroes." Over the years, standing on the frontlines of God's medical outreach without thought of commendation or acclaim, they quietly epitomize the mission of the CME/LLU School of Medicine. Certainly these physicians and their fellow alumni have brought distinction and great honor to their alma mater and a fulfilling kind of pride to Harold Shryock, one of their favorite mentors.

Harold firmly believed that, in heaven's perspective, Loma Linda University is *still* the College of Medical Evangelists. He had seen God's influences throughout the history of the institution. He witnessed critics proclaiming loud and long that the venture would fail. He observed controversies over accreditation and consolidation and sadly watched as some of the early participant's left because the sacrifice was just too great. But among those who remained, he never even *heard* the word "sacrifice." Instead, the declaration "faith" echoed from their lips as the next day's train delivered one more patient, the next medical class filled, and new graduates passed their state board examinations.

"The pioneers' faith was based on their conviction that the institution had an important role to play in fulfilling the Gospel Commission," Harold insisted. As clouds of uncertainty hovered over the struggling institution, it really had only one basis for optimism: Pioneers perceived that the Loma Linda enterprise operated under a Divine mandate. This was God's institution!

Harold Shryock died on March 3, 2004, following a brief illness. He looked forward to being reunited with his beloved Daisy in the hereafter. Patti had her father's casket covered with daisies. He had lived 97 years, 10 months, and 19 days. During his memorial service, Randy Roberts, senior pastor of the University Church of Seventh-day Adventists, displayed Shryock's Bible and, referring to the underlining, highlighting, and notes throughout, stated, "Whoever owned this Bible . . . was certainly a friend of God." Roberts then quoted three of the passages, including a statement Jesus made to Martha in John 11:25: "I am the resurrection, and the life: he that believeth in me, though he were dead, yet shall he live."

Although of moderate height, Shryock stood tall among Loma Linda's giants. When he pondered the providential heritage of Loma Linda and re-called how it unfolded right before his eyes . . . when he reviewed the eternal influence of its graduates who've gone to the ends of the earth . . . and when he recalled the part he played in the school's mission, Dr. Harold Shryock could only exclaim, "What hath God wrought!"

THE END

Whatever Happened to . . . ?

Wilton Thomas—Harold's college friend E. Wilton Thomas, the room-mate who introduced him to Daisy Bagwell in 1926, became a physician (CME: 1933) and opened a family practice in Colton, California. Harold remained ever grateful to Wilton for introducing him to his future wife—an act Shryock felt was providential.

Alfred Wical—The young man who took Harold Shryock and Lawrence Skinner on a vacation to Yosemite in the summer of 1927, riding in the Model-T Ford, became a radiologist (CME: 1941), practicing in Glendale, California.

Lawrence Skinner—Harold Shryock's best friend, Lawrence Skinner, became an associate secretary of the Missionary Volunteer Department at the General Conference of Seventh-day Adventists. Shryock stayed in his home on business trips to Washington, D. C. He and Skinner were friends since they were teenagers.

Alfred and Stella Shryock—Alfred Shryock, who served as dean of the School of Medicine from 1914 to 1915 and chair of the Department of Anatomy for most of his career, died at the age of 79 on January 3, 1950. At the time of his passing, he was the only member of the faculty who had taught every medical student who ever attended CME.

One of Alfred's most lasting contributions to the world of medical education is the Alfred Shryock Museum of Embryology—an amazing collection of human embryos and fetuses ranging in age from three weeks gestation to full term. He subjected one series of specimens to a special procedure that turned the tissue transparent. He then stained the calcium deposits in the developing bones in order to display the skeletal structure as it matures. The results show the complete skeleton developing in place inside the unborn child. These incredible teaching aids have been studied by thousands of medical students over the years.

In 1960, CME named the anatomy building, constructed in 1936 on the northwest corner of the basic sciences quadrangle, Alfred Shryock Hall.

Stella Shryock became known as a competent histologist in her own right. She worked late whenever necessary. Popular with her students, she circulated in the laboratory to help them individually. She prepared many of her own microscopic slides for her classes. In 1955, with other CME pioneers, local dignitaries, and church officials, Stella represented her husband at the fiftieth anniversary celebration of the founding of the institution. She died in 1971 at age 95.

Patricia Shryock Wallace—Patti lives with her husband, G. Carleton Wallace, M.D., near Corona, California, where Wallace is an orthopedic surgeon. The Wallaces are members of the Loma Linda University Adventist Health Sciences Center Councilors, a group that assists the president in developing and enhancing the university as an institution of higher education and service. The councilors also provide counsel, support, and leadership in the financing of university projects, and promote the university in the business and professional community.

Edwin F. Shryock—In 1962 Ed graduated from the Loma Linda University School of Dentistry and established a general practice in Santa Maria, California. In 1964 he expanded his work and became a part-time assistant professor at his alma mater. In 1969 he became a research associate at the School of Dentistry, at the same time working on his master's degree. In 1972 Edwin F. Shryock, D.D.S., M.S., became chair of the Department of Occlusion and Fixed Prosthodontics at the University of Florida. In July 1997 he returned to Loma Linda University School of Dentistry and became a professor in the Department of Restorative Dentistry. Ed is the father of two sons and three daughters. The Shryock legacy in Loma Linda now embraces three generations!